The Holy Spirit, Women, *and* Mission

"Dr. Julie Ma offers a vital exploration of the evolving role of women in ministry, with a particular focus on Asia. Blending personal insight with compelling stories of influential women—focusing primarily on those from the last century—Ma brings to life their work and experiences that have helped shape the church. Her integration of biblical perspectives often highlights the tension between cultural barriers and divine calling, while illustrating how these women, empowered by faith, found the strength and courage to persevere. Ma underscores their lasting contributions and urges the church to recognize, engage, and support such ministries as they confront the complex challenges of the twenty-first century."

—**KATHALEEN REID-MARTINEZ,**
Provost, Oral Roberts University

"I welcome this authentic account of the experience of Christian women outside the West by one who is representative of such women and has wide global experience. Dr. Julie Ma has brought together a wealth of data and stories of such women's ministry on several continents while also recounting their challenges in fulfilling their callings to evangelize, lead, and teach. The evidence in this book and the author's arguments will encourage many other women to live into the freedom of the Spirit, which is indiscriminately poured out on both women and men."

—**KIRSTEEN KIM,**
Paul E. Pierson Professor of World Christianity, Fuller Theological Seminary

"This insightful exploration of women's roles in leadership and ministry brilliantly highlights their invaluable contributions to the church and society. The case studies presented shed light on the challenges faced by women in the Global South and emphasize God's call for all people, regardless of gender. With rich examples of perseverance and faith, this work is a vital resource for understanding and promoting equality and empowerment in spiritual leadership. Highly recommended!"

—**OPOKU ONYINAH,**
Former Chairman, The Church of Pentecost

"Although there are now an increasing number of studies focusing on women in mission, few have been written from a Pentecostal perspective and with an emphasis on the Asian context. Dr. Julie Ma's book, which helps to fill a gap, should therefore be warmly welcomed. Of particular interest is Ma's argument that to be able to take on leadership roles, again and again, women have had to overcome strong gender biases within their respective social-ecclesial cultures. This breaking of glass ceilings can often be traceable to the Spirit's empowerment in Pentecostal theology. I heartily commend this significant contribution to our understanding of the role of Pentecostal women in mission."

—**HWA YUNG,**
Bishop Emeritus, The Methodist Church in Malaysia

The Holy Spirit, Women, *and* Mission

JULIE C. MA

Foreword by Cecil M. Robeck Jr.

PICKWICK *Publications* • Eugene, Oregon

THE HOLY SPIRIT, WOMEN, AND MISSION

Pickwick Publications
An Imprint of Wipf and Stock Publishers
199 W. 8th Ave., Suite 3
Eugene, OR 97401

www.wipfandstock.com

PAPERBACK ISBN: 979-8-3852-3918-4
HARDCOVER ISBN: 979-8-3852-3919-1
EBOOK ISBN: 979-8-3852-3920-7

Cataloguing-in-Publication data:

Names: Ma, Julie C. author.

Title: The Holy Spirit, Women, and Mission / Julie C. Ma.

Description: Eugene, OR: Pickwick Publications, 2026 | Includes bibliographical references and index.

Identifiers: ISBN 979-8-3852-3918-4 (paperback) | ISBN 979-8-3852-3919-1 (hardcover) | ISBN 979-8-3852-3920-7 (ebook)

Subjects: LCSH: Women in church work—Pentecostal churches. | Pentecostalism—Asia. | Christianity—Asia. | Pentecostal women.

Classification: BX8762.A85 M3 2026 (paperback) | BX8762.A85 (ebook)

02/17/26

To the Elder Jonggi Kang,
Taepyung Holiness Church, Tongyoung, Korea
for his amazing spiritual fatherhood through my theological study, missionary work, and teaching ministry

Contents

Foreword

Professor Julie Ma begins this work by quoting from the "Word of the Lord" that came to the prophet (Joel 2:28–29), which the apostle Peter quoted from memory on the Day of Pentecost (Acts 2:17–19). It was a promise from the God of Israel. One day, God promised, "I will pour out my Spirit on all flesh"; when that happens, "Your sons and your daughters shall prophesy." Pentecostals say that they believe this "Word" or "Prophecy" as coming from the Lord, and you might think that they would honor all who receive the Spirit equally. But their actions speak more loudly than do their affirmations. Professor Ma notes that there is often inconsistency when considering the disparity between the treatment and recognition we give our sons and what we offer to our daughters. We value our sons more than our daughters when recognizing them as recipients of the prophetic Spirit. I hope that you will pardon me if I say that our response is not very Pentecostal, nor do I believe that it is even Christian.

One paragraph stands out in *The Apostolic Faith*, published by the Azusa Street Mission in 1908. It reads,

> Contrary to the Scriptures, a woman should not have her part in the salvation work to which God has called her. We have no right to lay a straw in her way, but to be men of holiness, purity, and virtue, to hold up the standard, and to encourage the woman in her work. God will honor and bless us as never before. It is the same Holy Spirit in the woman as in the man.[1]

If we believed the "Word of the Lord" given to us through the prophet Joel, and repeated through the apostle Peter, we might find more consistent ways to acknowledge the "Word of the Lord" in Joel 2 and Acts 2 and to honor the sentiment that is expressed in this early Pentecostal passage. However, it seems that we have allowed our various cultures to dictate the

1. Untitled article, *The Apostolic Faith* 1.12 (January 1908), §2.4.

meaning of the "Word of the Lord" instead of recognizing it for what it was when it was first spoken in a very different culture.

This point recalls another passage we love to repeat but do not seem to believe. "If God is for us, who is against us?" (Rom 8:31). When God pours out the Spirit upon our daughters, and calls them into ministry, it should be clear that God is for them. Yet, we balk and stand against them and what God has called and gifted them to do. We tend to focus on verses like 1 Cor 14:34b, "Women should be silent in the churches," to justify our actions. We strip such a verse from its original context and culture and foolishly apply it using the logic of our biased contemporary culture.

Julie Ma has observed such claims firsthand. Drawing from her extensive mission work in South Korea, the Philippines, the UK, and the US, she tells the stories of some women, especially from the Global South. These are women God has called, but because of ecclesial policies informed by contemporary cultures, they often lack access to the resources, opportunities, and positions that might be theirs if only they were our sons instead of our daughters.

Even among Pentecostals, historians find that research on the contributions of Pentecostal women is very difficult to document, and often it is impossible to do because we know these women only as the spouse of a man who is named, while their name does not appear. I have been frustrated, for example, to read many early reports regarding Brother Junk and his wife or another named man and unnamed wife, as though naming her might detract from his reputation.

What Professor Ma does in this book is document the issue of the unequal treatment of our sons and daughters who have received the same prophetic Spirit, as well as other issues that appear in various parts of the Global South, especially in Asia. She looks at the social systems found in various cultures, thereby demonstrating how women are often treated as inferior to men in value, as second-class people, or as non-persons. In this way, they are dehumanized. Using biographical narratives, she highlights the work of three specific women, Jashil Choi in South Korea, Elva Vanderbout in the Philippines, and Huldah Buntain in India, to demonstrate how God used them despite challenges and obstacles others set.

Among these examples, Julie has interwoven her own story as a theological educator, evangelist, church planter, and preacher from the Global South, as she has ministered in many places worldwide. Whether these women ministered in an animist culture, such as in the Philippines, a

Confucian culture that still dominates Korea, or the Hindu culture of India, Ma points to the accomplishments these women achieved through the gifts they received from God. That said, she also acknowledges the contributions of certain men, who recognized the gifts of these women and supported them as they experienced success on their own.

Elva Vanderbout began her ministry by working alone among children in a mountain community of the Philippines that other missionaries feared entering. She expanded her ministry by reaching out to the parents of the children and then traveling to other villages to teach the Bible and engage in a ministry full of signs and wonders. Ultimately, she established an orphanage and schools and built a church from the ground up. She then turned the church leadership over to a man, who respected her work. In the end, the two were married.

Yonggi Cho recognized the leadership and support his mother-in-law, Jashil Choi, gave him. Not only did she establish Yoido's Prayer Mountain, she also counseled Cho to ignore the surrounding culture and establish cell groups, most of which are now led by women God had called.

Upon their arrival in India, Mark and Huldah Buntain worked as a team. They were constantly engaged in evangelization but are best known for developing an essential and fruitful social ministry. Upon Mark's death, Huldah took the ministry that they had begun, a feeding program, schools, and a hospital, to new heights through her God-given leadership.

Professor Ma eventually supplements these biographical sketches with several other names, including Seenok Ahn and her husband, Ki Seuk Ahn, who began their work in North Korea and later in South Korea. There, they founded a thriving Foursquare Church. Trinidad (Esperanza) Seleky graduated from Fuller Theological Seminary before serving the General Council of the Assemblies of God in the Philippines as treasurer, teaching at the Asia Pacific Theological Seminary, and starting many social ministries. Virgie Cruz is a Filipina who became an international evangelist. She held many crusades and worked in community outreach. To these names, she adds many others.

The achievements of these women are in keeping with those of other women whose stories we read in the pages of Scripture. What Professor Ma has done is to make *a call for justice* in the treatment of our daughters, particularly the treatment of those daughters whom God has called and equipped for ministry. The women she has mentioned underwent undue hardships. Should they not have received the same support, resources, opportunities, and positions we make available to our sons? Will we continue to be led by our biased cultures, or should the "Word of the Lord" also dictate how we relate to our daughters?" Her overview of the cultural biases against women in a range of Asian countries should be sufficient to prick the consciences of men everywhere and arouse them to action when they hear the facts of female mistreatment. I hope that the readers of Professor Ma's account will be touched by the realities around them, even in Pentecostal churches.

Cecil M. Robeck, Jr.
Senior Professor of Church History and Ecumenics
Special Assistant to the President for Ecumenical Relations
Fuller Theological Seminary
Pasadena, California

Acknowledgments

I WOULD FIRST LIKE to express my gratitude to my spouse, Wonsuk Ma, who is also my academic partner. He has provided support, inspiration, and direction. He made a significant contribution to this book for improvement. The second individual is July Gilliland, a longtime friend who carefully read the text to improve it. The third group is Wipf and Stock's editorial team, who thoroughly reviewed the text.

The second category consists of the journal publishers who consented to my earlier research to be included in their books and magazines. For this book, they were updated and changed.

Asia Pacific Theological Seminary for its permission for:

- "Asian Women and Pentecostal Ministry," *Asian Journal of Pentecostal Studies* (2005) 129–46.
- "Korean Pentecostal Spirituality: A Case Study of Jashil Choi," *Asian Journal of Pentecostal Studies* 5:2 (2002) 235–54.

Oxford Center for Mission Studies for its permission for:

- "The Role of Christian Women in the Global South," *Transformation: An International Journal of Holistic Mission Studies* 31:3 (July 2014) 194–206.

Overseas Ministry Study Center for its permission for:

- "Touching Lives of People Through the Holistic Mission Work of the Buntains in Calcutta, India," *International Bulletin of Mission Research* 40:1 (Jan. 2016) 72–83.

Asia Graduate School of Theology for its permission for:

- "Elva Vanderbout: A Woman Pioneer of Pentecostal Mission Among Igorot," *Journal of Asian Mission* 3 (2001) 121–32.
- "Women at Yoido Full Gospel Church: Pentecostalism in a Confucian Society," *Journal of Asian Mission* 19:1 (May 2018) 35–57.

Bible College of Malaysia for its permission for:

- "The Spirit-Empowered Ministry of Pentecostal Women," *Malaysian Pentecostal Journal* 2:4 (2024) 43–66.

Wipf & Stock Publishers for its permission for:

- "Changing Image: Women in Asian Pentecostalism," in *Women in Pentecostal-Charismatic Leadership*, edited by Estrelda Alexander and Amos Yong, 203–14. Eugene, OR: Pickwick, 2009.

Oral Roberts University Press for its permission for:

- "Women at Yoido Full Gospel Church: Pentecostalism in a Confucian Context," in *Human Sexuality and the Holy Spirit: Spirit-Empowered Perspective*, edited by Wonsuk Ma and Kathaleen Reid-Martinez, 267–84. Tulsa, OK: Oral Roberts University Press, 2019.

My children make up the third group. My first son, Woolim, and his wife, Shiloah, are devoted to God's mission work. They left Manila to start a church in Seoul. Their dedication to God's work is admirable. It gives me much encouragement. It challenged my mission thinking. Boram, my second son, is currently pursuing a master's degree in counseling. His goal is to become a great counselor empowered by the Spirit. Ultimately, it serves as a mission for those needing inspirational guidance. I am reminded of our experience of God's lead when I watch him follow his course.

Julie C. Ma
Spring 2025

Introduction

JOEL'S PROPHECY CLARIFIES GOD'S plan for both men and women, as noted in Acts 2:17–18:

"In the last days, I will pour out my spirit on all people. Your sons and daughters will prophesy, your young men will see visions, your old men will dream dreams. Even on my servants, both men and women, I will pour out my Spirit in those days, and they will prophesy."

According to these verses, God's order includes both men and women. Both are equally precious in his eyes because they are made in his likeness. However, in our society or even in a church setting, recognition and acceptance of women's leadership roles are not equal.

In every step of the stewardship process, women have a unique role in the public, familial, and private domains. Women in the Global South, however, confront difficulties. In the public sphere, for instance, women's access to resources, opportunities, and leadership positions has been restricted in many cultures and nations. Defining their identity in a particular social context is the biggest obstacle for women. Cultural customs are difficult to abandon, and the way women are perceived and treated in many regions of Asia, Africa, and Latin America continues to be a complex problem. In many areas of Asia, for instance, a woman's identity is derived from her spouse or children, and she is still referred to today as so and so's mother or wife in many locations. As a result, her name is less well-known and rarely used.

A few case studies in India, the Philippines, and Korea will be reviewed, to better understand women's significant roles more clearly. In the Global South, there has been intense discussion about women's ordination. Women are frequently ordained as ministers in Pentecostal churches in the West, and evidence of a divine call for service was frequently used as the evaluation criterion rather than credentials. Because of this, the early Pentecostal movement did not have a problem with women being ordained. However, this ostensibly innovative idea was tested as Pentecostal institutionalization occurred and Western Pentecostal missionaries arrived in Asia. In the initial three decades of the Korean Assemblies of God, for instance, fewer than three women ministers were ordained nationwide compared to over a thousand ordained men. And, despite having the same supernatural calling to serve the church, women ministers continue to live as second-class ministers because the male-dominated culture has stifled their freedom. For instance, although Pentecostals are often much more receptive to women being ordained than other conventional churches, the Church of God in Christ, the most well-known African American Pentecostal denomination, does not ordain women.

Even though women encountered obstacles and difficulties because they were presumed to be unequal to men in their leadership and capability roles, no one could prevent or oppose their involvement in God's ministry when God empowered them with the Spirit and used them in extraordinary ways. Chapter 1 discusses the leadership development of women in academic circles. They were involved in various academic exercises such as producing books and articles, taking up their role in leading conferences, and presenting papers etc. Chapter 2 delineates Jashil Choi's spiritual life and ministry locally and overseas. She was highly respected due to her exemplary spiritual life, dedication, and commitment to God's service. She lived a life of prayer and fasting, frequently at night, and her intense prayer focus helped her through every difficult time in her life and ministry. Despite the fierce criticism of some church officials, she was determined to establish a prayer mountain with a clear focus on fasting after witnessing the power of prayer. Despite every adverse situation, her will was so powerful that even Yonggi Cho, the founding pastor of Yoido Full Gospel Church, could not stop her. Choi is the mother-in-law of Cho.

Chapter 3 illustrates the fantastic work of the Holy Spirit through an American woman missionary among the Kankana-ey tribal people. The Assemblies of God began working with the Kankana-eys in 1947. One American missionary woman, Elva Vanderbout, carried on the ministry with a few local leaders. Before she started working there, neither national workers nor missionaries from the Assemblies of God had attempted mountain ministry. Vanderbout delivered a unique Christian message: God's might. Churches were established due to the gospel of supernatural power and its manifestation, and the Assemblies of God's mountain mission was successfully begun and carried on.

Chapter 4 deals with how Christianity challenged the long-standing cultural norm in gender-biased Korean society by encouraging education and social roles for women. The idea that men were superior to women and could accomplish more was one facet of Confucian thought, emphasizing the unequal status of men and women. Its effects persisted in Korean society until recently, as boys were preferred over girls, ultimately leading to a gender imbalance in the population. The influence of David Yonggi Cho's Yoido Full Gospel Church shows how the growth of Pentecostalism significantly strengthened this latter cultural issue. The most crucial program was Cho's audacious decision to appoint women as the leaders of his popular cell group structure. This replaced his original intention to assign males to leadership roles in the cells, which was surprisingly met with resistance from female lay leaders. The current senior pastor, Younghoon Lee, supports the predominantly female leadership of the cell group structure.

Chapter 5 describes Mark and Huldah Buntain, appointed from the Assemblies of God in America to Calcutta, India, who served the people in Calcutta wholeheartedly. They started their work with a goal and deep commitment to reach Calcutta for Christ and transform people's lives. After a short period there, they quickly concluded that the city offered no hope to the hungry, the hurting, the deformed children, and many other groups. They began a feeding program after learning that parents had left countless street children behind. A few years later, they constructed a hospital and a school. Other ministries were progressively founded to address people's concerns and offer hope.

Chapter 6 delineates the significant impact of women in Asia's education, churches, and spiritual life. Their influence has been much more significant with their unique spiritual abilities and unwavering dedication. However, because their culture has frequently overlooked women's leadership abilities and traits in society and the church, although globalization has improved women's responsibilities in some ways, full acknowledgment is still relatively low.

The purpose of chapter 7 is to examine the evolving role of women in society, particularly in Asia, and to talk about how women are portrayed in both biblical and modern cultural contexts. I will examine the following underlying question: To what extent can we anticipate that women's roles will be increased and changed in the church today, particularly in Asia? This subject presents significant potential and challenges for the church.

Chapter 8 highlights Pentecostal women who have boldly assumed leadership positions within the church and actively advanced God's kingdom. Their involvement in several ministries that have assisted the impoverished, disenfranchised, and abandoned in society further demonstrates their extraordinary understanding of human needs and the Spirit's guidance. They went above and beyond in their influence and accomplishments. These case studies will also emphasize their challenges, particularly when viewed through conventional theological and ecclesiastical perspectives. They show the Holy Spirit's transformative power by overcoming these and other challenges.

1

The Role of Christian Women in the Global South

Many people in the churches in the Global South (henceforth "the Southern Church"), including myself, ponder upon the exact meaning and implications of the southward shift of the center of global Christianity. A particular question is raised: Are there any significant roles for the Southern Church to play? If so, what would they be, especially in a global setting? God has drawn and positioned both men and women into his kingdom to fulfill God-given purposes, encompassing all levels of social life. Women's contributions, therefore, are intended not only for local levels (e.g., local church settings) but also in global settings by exercising their leadership roles and sometimes by partnering with men.

In this study, I will survey images of women in the Global South and argue for a need to restore the biblical understanding of womanhood. I will reflect on my personal experiences throughout my intellectual journey, which is not an ideal model and is still in the making. Nonetheless, I hope such will serve as small windows through which fellow women will come to understand their unique and yet significant roles in shaping global Christianity.

Two presumptions are considered for this discussion: (1) Global Christianity is now a "Southern" religion, with more than two thirds of the world's Christians now living in the Southern Hemisphere, and (2) the majority of these Christians are women, and yet, various factors, including socio-cultural elements, often hamper their God-called roles.

WHAT DOES THE SHIFT OF THE GLOBAL CHRISTIAN CENTER MEAN?

As Philip Jenkins asserts, the influences for the new Christianity will come from the Global South so that it will be remarkably dissimilar from Christianity under Western dominance. It will be more indigenous, evangelical, Bible-oriented, and Pentecostal/Charismatic.[1] Furthermore, the era of Western Christianity has passed within our lifetimes, and the day of Southern Christianity is dawning. The fact of change itself is undeniable: it has happened and will continue to happen. So, little did we notice this momentous change that was barely mentioned in all the media hoopla surrounding the end of the second millennium.[2]

Christianity in the West is declining, and it will have to reinvent itself to make it relevant and ensure its continuing existence. Often, one can observe a decrease in church attendance, and many historic and magnificent church buildings are turned into tourist attractions. From the onslaught of secularism and religious pluralism, Christianity's place in the public sphere is continuously shrinking, while traditional Christian values are constantly being challenged by changing social standards. The sexuality debates in the Anglican Church are a good example. The anger expressed within and without the Church of England at the failed vote against women bishops may further marginalize the church as an irrelevant, archaic institution. The Christian population's constant decline and the church's eroding role in society have cast the Western church in a defensive and survival mode. The church, primarily being more than a spiritual and faith community, will have to discover and harness divine resources entrusted to them. God intends to pour out his life-giving Spirit as promised to his people. Isaiah 44:3–4 reads, "For I will pour water on the thirsty land, and streams on the dry ground; I will pour out my Spirit on your offspring, and my blessing on your descendants. They will spring up like grass in a meadow, like poplar trees by flowing streams." A careful review of church history gives us hope that a revival is God's way of restoring his church to vibrant life. With the exponential growth of Christianity in the Southern Hemisphere and its increasing influence in the West, mainly through ever-increasing migration, the energy and spiritual resources from the South can be a critical spiritual capital in the revival of the Western church. Knowing that the

1. Jenkins, *Next Christendom*, 68–73.
2. Jenkins, *Next Christendom*, 68–73.

global Christian center has shifted, the next step is to discuss the church's challenges in the Global South.

CHALLENGES OF THE CHURCH IN THE GLOBAL SOUTH

It has been argued that the church in the Global South has been called to play a historic role at the global level. In some countries in the South, the growth of Christianity is coupled with social and economic advancement. Christians here have rightly perceived increasing human and financial capacities as a missionary gift. The stewardship of resources is guided by the teaching of the Lord as recorded in Matt 25:24–29:

> Then the man who had received the one talent came. "Master," he said, "I know that you are a hard man, harvesting where you have not sown and gathering where you have not scattered seed. So, I was afraid and went out and hid your talent in the ground. See, here is what belongs to you." His master replied, "You wicked, lazy servant! So, you knew that I harvest where I have not sown and gather where I have not scattered seed? Well then, you should have deposited my money with the bankers so I would have received it back with interest. So, take the bag of gold from him and give it to the one with the ten bags. For whoever has will be given more, and they will have an abundance. Whoever does not have, even what they have, will be taken from them."

The passage contains the rebuke of the master addressing the failing stewardship of a servant. Stewardship presumes an awareness of the resources entrusted by the valid owner—a proper understanding of the master's instruction springs from a proper relationship. Knowing the mind of his master, he is to dispense the master's resources for his benefit correctly. Burying it is regarded as abandoning stewardship or the steward's expected responsibility. The offense is so grave that its punishment leaves no provision for a second chance. Even if one reads and becomes aware of this entrusted nature of every gift, including our own life, it is easy to completely ignore this and act no differently from the "lazy and evil servant." As the center of the gravity of global Christianity has shifted and continues its southward move, the church in the South is called to discover God-entrusted gifts/resources/opportunities and to mobilize and deploy them for God's kingdom.

Women play a unique role in almost every stage of the stewardship process, both in the private, family, and public spheres. At the same time, women in the Global South face unique challenges. For example, in the public dimension, many cultures and societies have limited women from accessing resources, opportunities, and leadership roles. The foremost challenge for women is establishing their identity in a given social setting. Cultural practices are hard to die, and how women are viewed and treated in many parts of Asia, Africa, and Latin America remains a formidable challenge. For example, in many parts of Asia, a woman's identity comes from her husband or children; still, in many places, she is called so and so's wife or mother. Consequently, her name is seldom used and thus is less known. Surprisingly, I discovered it in Korea in the church, where women are mostly called by their names.

Women's ordination has been hotly debated in the Global South. In the West, Pentecostal churches regularly ordain women as ministers. Often, the criterion for evaluation is not qualifications but the evidence of a divine call for service. For this reason, the ordination of women in the early Pentecostal movement was not an issue. However, this seemingly revolutionary concept was tested severely during Pentecostal institutionalization; it was also challenged when Western Pentecostal missionaries arrived on Asian soil. Can Pentecostal women receive equal treatment in ministry and have the same opportunity as men to receive ordination? Could this be applied to all Pentecostal traditions, including those in Asia?

In the first thirty years of the Korean Assemblies of God, there were fewer than three ordained women ministers throughout the country, while the ordained men numbered more than one thousand. (Some large Korean Presbyterian churches still do not allow women's ordination.) Although its Constitution provided for the ordination of women, the Korean Assemblies of God placed an unusual number of restrictions on women, including requirements to be single or be a widow. It was not until recently that many of these restrictions were removed. In other Asian countries, the ordination of women is not permitted. Women ministers, possessing the same divine call to serve Christ's church as men, still live as second-class ministers, as the male-dominant culture has suppressed the freedom found in Christ and his Spirit.

For example, the Church of God in Christ, the most prominent African American Pentecostal denomination, does not ordain women, even though Pentecostals are generally far more open to women's ordination than other traditional churches. Women can only be substitutes for male pastors:

> In the absence of a pastor and with official approval, a woman can "act" in the role of pastor. Official approval may come from the pastor who designates which woman will serve while he is absent from his church. In the event of a vacancy of the pastorate, a district superintendent or jurisdictional bishop may authorize a woman to act in the role of pastor until a permanent appointment can be made. But she cannot assume the title of "pastor." She may be called by other titles, such as, "missionary," "mother," or "shepherdess." If the woman is (pastor), she must use the "covering" of a man—a husband, father, brother, uncle, son or nephew—in order to carry out pastoral and other chief leadership roles.[3]

Another practice shaped by the teachings of Confucianism in Asia is that men are described as the "sky," while women are the "earth." This is not just a yin-yang relationship, with its different but complementary roles, but a matter of injustice and discrimination. For example, even today, in some homes, mothers and children do not eat at the same table when there is a guest of the father. They wait until the father and his guest have finished their meals. Any leftovers are for the mother and her children. This notion of social values leads some families to dress girls in boy's clothes or give a girl a boy's name to express their regret that they are not boys. A striking fact is that even after the women have grown up, they still behave like men. This practice has reinforced the notion of male superiority over females in many societies.

In some religious settings, such as Islam, women must publicly cover their faces and bodies. Moreover, women have seldom questioned this practice due to solid religious pressures and orientation. Even if this is accepted as a cultural practice, limitations placed on women for education, employment, and other opportunities are more than a cultural issue—it is a justice issue.

In some nations, female rape victims are imprisoned for adultery while their attackers go free.[4] "Honor killings" of women and young girls are also on the rise. A woman does not have to be guilty of doing something immoral to be killed. Her father, husband, brothers, and uncles may kill

3. Dabney, *What It Means to Pray Through*, 24. Dabney's prayer ministry and role as "national evangelist" contributed to her husband's success and advancement in COGIC.

4. Ehrenreich, "For Women," 13.

her simply because she is the subject of gossip. No one knows the exact number of honor killings, but in just one region of these nations, 350 young women—some as young as twelve—were murdered in one year. The preferred method of killing women to restore honor to the family is to burn them alive or throw acid on them.[5]

Such a notion of women's inferiority is ingrained in many religious values, including Judaism. In ancient Judaism, male members of the society participated in Jewish festivals held in the temple. Segregation has also continued in synagogue worship for millennia. "By the second century after Christ, archaeology suggests that the synagogues kept women in screened second-floor galleries that they entered by a back door."[6] The rabbis required ten Jewish males for a local synagogue to be constituted. Even though there was no base in Scripture, this religious tradition sends a clear signal to women: "You do not count."[7] The following section will discuss the views from biblical texts.

WHAT THE BIBLE TEACHES ABOUT HUMAN SEXUALITY

The Old Testament

It is appropriate to look at Scripture and how it views gender. God created equality in man and woman according to his image, although their roles differ. In fact, "man" (or "human") in Gen 1:27 is used as a collective noun. This value of equality is not only applied to gender, race, and ethnic background, but also to the poor and the rich. Human sinful nature and culture distorted this principle of equal value from the earliest history. The human tendency is to build a social system that would protect one's power, status, and privilege, both individually and corporately. If a society is organized around wealth, education, and social status, a notion of equality has less chance. This is far more than meeting basic human needs, an essential goal of human development. The Tower of Babel in Gen 11:1–9 is a prime example of human temptation to build one's ego ever higher.

Now, the whole world has one language and everyday speech. As men moved eastward, they found a plain in Shinar and settled there. It notes,

5. *Nightline* by ABC News, transcript from television broadcasts, March 1980.

6. Spencer, *Beyond the Curse*, 49.

7. Hyman, "Other Half," 239.

> They said to each other, "Come, let's make bricks and bake them thoroughly." They used brick instead of stone and tar for mortar. Then they said, "Come, let us build ourselves a city, with a tower that reaches to the heavens, so that we may make a name for ourselves; otherwise we will be scattered over the face of the whole earth." But the LORD came down to see the city and the town the men were building. The LORD said, "If as one people speaking the same language, they have begun to do this, then nothing they plan to do will be impossible for them. Come, let us go down and confuse their language so they will not understand each other." So, the LORD scattered them over all the earth, and they stopped building the city. That is why it was called Babel—because the LORD confused the language of the whole world. From there the LORD scattered them over the face of the whole earth.

This portrays the human tendency to build a status symbol and expand their territory or influence with every available resource and skill. This enhances one's sense of security. We are no better than the people in the Plain of Babel: our towers are perhaps subtler than the Tower of Babel. Our towers are hierarchies, pyramid charts, and structures that give some people more value than others. Our hierarchical structures begin in pride and self-assertion, not in God or his word, and end in injustice.[8] In this social order, the value of men and women is not equal but hierarchical.[9]

Paul's Teaching

On the one hand, Paul admonishes, "Women should remain silent in the churches . . ." (1 Cor 14:34); on the other hand, he tells women to pray and prophesy (1 Cor 11:5). One can easily detect that Paul was in a situation where he could not help but give such instructions. First Corinthians 14:3 explains that prophecy is meant to edify the body of Christ, and its function is like that of teaching and exhorting to correct, console, and encourage. Paul perhaps intended to allow women to do all these in public.[10]

Joel's prophecy helps us understand the purpose of God for both man and woman: "In the last days, God says, I will pour out my Spirit on all people. Your sons and daughters will prophesy, your young men will see visions, and your old men will dream dreams. Even on my servants, both

8. Cunningham, "How We Know What We Believe," 29–44.

9. Giles, *Trinity and Subordinationism*, 185.

10. Ma, *When the Spirit Meets the Spirits*, 113–15.

men and women, I will pour out my Spirit in those days, and they will prophesy" (Acts 2:17–18). These scriptures indicate that God included man and woman in his order.[11] Both are created according to his image and, thus, are equally valuable before him. Only sinful culture allows practices of inequality. This does not deny the different roles of male and female, which are part of God's creation order.

Can the church equally utilize women and men in its public ministry? In some Asian churches, this matter is hotly debated, and it is not a settled matter of how much women can exercise their call to ministry. My observation and experience inform me that women are reasonably permitted to work within the boundary of a local church, but even then, they are often far under-used. It is noted in the Bible that the gifts and callings of God are irrevocable (Rom 11:29) and intended for his glory.

The Importance of Women in Jesus' Life

Jesus was conceived and born only through the agency of a woman, Mary. No matter how the Greek understanding of the "headship" of men implies their strength, their reproduction cannot be achieved without women's agency. During Jesus' earthly ministry, women showed their untiring faithfulness to him. Women were with the Lord at critical moments, including his death, resurrection, and ascension. After the resurrection, Jesus appeared first to Mary Magdalene. Women were the first to locate the empty tomb. Jesus told them to go and tell the others that he was alive. So, women were the first to hear Jesus' command to go and tell the good news.

Jesus had unforgettable experiences when two women anointed him. In the final week in Lazarus's house before his death, Mary anointed Jesus (John 12:1–8). Several days later, another woman entered the house where Jesus was eating. She poured an alabaster jar's content of costly ointment over his head. Jesus' commendation of her devotion was exceptional, and her act would be spoken about wherever the gospel was preached (Matt 26:6–13). In dealing with women's faithfulness to Jesus in the following section, I reflect on my own Christian journey and academic experience and make observations both in the local and global setting.

11. Scanzoni and Setta, "Women in Evangelical, Holiness, and Pentecostal Traditions," 256.

REFLECTION OF ACADEMIC EXERCISE OF WOMEN SCHOLARS FROM THE GLOBAL SOUTH

This section illustrates areas where a woman's contribution can be significant. The discussion also presents the challenges and obstacles women face and overcome in a particular social setting.

Theological Education

My career as a theological educator includes a regional denominational school in Asia for a decade and, at present, an institution created by and for preparing regional and global leaders from the Southern Hemisphere. Without diminishing the importance of leaders at the local and national levels, a critical need at this level of leadership training will determine the sustained growth and maturity of the churches in Africa, Asia, Latin America, and Eastern/Central Europe. It will ultimately determine the future expansion and shape of global Christianity.

My teaching career began in a Pentecostal graduate school in the Philippines in 1996, right after completing my doctoral degree.[12] The school's student body represented over twenty countries, including non-Asians. The faculty also represented seven nations, both Asian and Western. Teaching was always a challenge for an Asian woman. Perhaps a similar experience is of a Japanese woman scholar, Eiko Takamizawa, who had been on the teaching faculty for fourteen years at Torch Trinity Graduate University in Seoul, Korea.[13] A handful of students in the mission studies program had already gained field experiences in cross-cultural contexts, while others were preparing for mission work. Often, such a mixture in the student body provides a rare opportunity to learn from each other by sharing empirical experiences. Various local perspectives are shared, shaping a more extensive global picture or global interactions. This mutual influence is analogous to the formation of ecclesiology through the relationship between the universal church and local churches.[14]

12. I taught different mission courses for ten years. Many students from numerous Asian and non-Asian countries undertook the mission program.

13. Eiko Takamizawa had been on the faculty, teaching missiology at the above-mentioned school for fourteen years, and she also regularly visited Londrina Biblical Seminary, Londrina, Brazil, to teach mission courses.

14. Julie Ma, personal diary.

My experience at the global level proved to be extremely rewarding and, at the same time, challenging. A brief description of the institution may provide a context: A small independent postgraduate research center was established by a network of mission practitioners, especially from the Global South, to prepare leaders from the South in Christian mission. Within the broader evangelical world, the institution and its network advocated and disseminated research on the holistic nature of the Christian gospel and mission. The British higher education framework allows the possibility of such a small institution, taking full advantage of more comprehensive resources, to produce an incredible output, be it in research or in training global leaders. More than 120 PhD students are enrolled, primarily part-time, representing almost all known Christian families worldwide with diverse research topics. The most rewarding experience is that every national and regional leader in their own right perseveres to complete their doctorate, and the fruit of their research makes a unique contribution to the world of mission studies. Although studies are often context-specific, these reflections on local engagements become the building blocks of future mission studies. The biggest challenge is how we, coming from a specific "Southern" context, can gain sufficient global insights to guide these leaders in their research. Being at the center of the Western university hub, the institution is constantly struggling to sustain the claim of the uniqueness of such research in traditional Western academia. I share this challenge on a personal level. Being a woman has come with an added advantage; many research topics are women-related, directly or indirectly. Subjects such as poverty, HIV/AIDS, education, human trafficking, and children at risk directly affect women, and their role in overcoming these social problems is critical. Even topics such as the church and state relationship, inter-religious issues, migration/refugees, community development, and other justice issues include many implications for women and their roles.[15]

For theological reflection to impact mission practices and the way mission is perceived, theological education has to take the reality of life seriously. Thus, the ideal profile of a theologian or theological educator is a reflective practitioner, often living and engaging in a particular social and local context. One must be genuinely local to contribute to making a global theology. It is particularly true if the future of theological formation is to

15. If visiting OCMS website on the front page, there is a section called "Resources" that has thesis abstracts. About one hundred theses written on various research areas are in the list.

reflect the realities of the places where Christianity is growing and spreading, i.e., the Global South.

Our continued theological embracement of Enlightenment thinking is a challenge because it makes it difficult for us to accept that the growing faith in the Global South is not asking permission from our modern paradigm to grow and develop as it wishes.[16] Rather, theologies of the Global South strongly criticize what Hwa Yung calls an "unengaged" Western theology.[17] As children of the Enlightenment, we distinguish between theory and practice. An encounter with theologies from the Global South will help us to understand that theology cannot and must not be separated from the concrete world. Truth cannot be separated from practice, and orthopraxis is as essential as orthodoxy. Theology must, therefore, be based on missional/missionary experience; that was how the theology of the early church came into being as a theoretical framework of conceptual thinking based on concrete mission experience: theological thinking must be missiological thinking to hold together practice and theory.[18]

The Creation of New Christian Knowledge

The European missiologist Knud Jorgensen warns, "Theology in the global South will dominate the next Christianity, although it may take on some strange forms; it is from this part of the world that renewal of theology and church life may come." He further argues that African theologian Kwame Bediako, from Ghana, says that African Christianity will probably "rescue our memories in recovering a primal Christian consciousness."[19] Bediako sees African Christianity as a rediscovery of biblical Christianity in an African context; particularly the experience of the transcendent in the midst of the immanent is one of the characteristics: God lives and acts and weeps and dances amid the world. Further, what is true about the African experience may also be witnessed by the liberated faith of Latin America—liberated in both a socio-political sense and in a deep, existential and religious sense. Alternatively, if we visit some open and house churches of China, we

16. Aano, "Church Going Glocal."
17. Yung, *Mangoes or Bananas*, 8.
18. Jorgensen, "Mission in the Post-Modern Society," 7.
19. Hartman, *Kwame Bediako*, 23.

will meet the same living, invigorating, shouting, praying, and infectious faith.[20]

We must write to let others hear about all these incredible experiences and reflections among dynamic Christian communities in the Global South. Literature travels much farther than people and remains much longer. It is where I found a great challenge as an Asian woman. First, my early education, perhaps Asian education in general, did not prepare me to be analytical or reflective. We were taught to reproduce existing knowledge. During my days in international institutional settings, I was trained and encouraged to produce my own understanding.[21] At the same time, I have also valued my Asian thinking and writing patterns, thus trying to express such narratives in an Asian way.

Although Western theological minds can lend helping hands in the process of theologization in the Global South, it will have to be insiders, i.e., Africans, Asians, Latin Americans, and Eastern and Central Europeans, who carry the burden of charting the theological future. We all need to heed Jenkins's crucial warning: "I somehow doubt that the Global South's contribution to theological inquiry will be confined to rhythmic dancing or handclapping."[22] The old dictum may ironically contain truth: "Publish or perish!"

Publishing

The dissemination of created knowledge can take various forms. The first and obvious one is publication. Monographs and scholarly articles can be published both in print form and online. It is encouraging to see a growing number of doctoral dissertations produced by reflective minds from the South. This used to take place in theological institutions in the West, but now research-based postgraduate programs have grown in number in Africa, Asia, and Latin America. Yet, as only a few of these studies find their way into publication, new studies from the new churches must fight an even more brutal battle. But on two fronts, positive signs are detected. One is the availability of modern communication technology. Even if a

20. Jorgensen, "Mission in the Post-Modern Society," 7.

21. I had a chance of exposure to a Western education environment for pursuing my further education in the Philippines and in America where my analytical thinking was shaped.

22. Jenkins, *Next Christendom*, 103.

study is not formally published, the internet provides a superb platform to share one's study. This can be housed on an institutional site or other public platforms. Search engines pick them up for broader visibility. Also increasingly available are online library sites hosting many studies that would have otherwise been unknown.[23] The other avenue is the traditional publication. Increasingly, established Western publishers have begun to include non-Western authors. A few publishers give priority to authors from the Global South.[24] Of course, now more publishers in Africa, Asia, Latin America, and Eastern Europe produce quality books for the world market. Modern technology has also helped to make these studies more visible and available through global market sites. This increasing availability applies to professional and academic journals.

Once publications are available, deep and meaningful engagements take place among like-minded theologians. The more I write and engage through dialogue, the more opportunities are created. It also opens new horizons to my knowledge, while interaction with other scholars provides continual challenges and new insights. Rosalee V. Ewell, a Latin American woman scholar, presented a paper in the Stott and Bediako Forum at Oxford Centre for Mission Studies, Oxford, UK, in June 2013. She has not only been involved in paper presentations but also in publishing articles on various interesting topics.[25]

One handy gift in this area is editing. Whether it is a journal or a volume with collected essays, editing creates a new space where the editor can encourage new authors from the South to join established (often Western) authors to share their knowledge on a common theme. I know the editors of some academic journals who are sensitive to encouraging those voices from the South to be heard.[26]

Thankfully, there has been movement on several fronts. First, the rise of contemporary communication technology has radically expanded spaces to share knowledge. Publishing media now includes institutional

23. For example, recently the World Council of Churches set up a new online library named the Global Digital Library on Theology and Ecumenism. It is "a multilingual online library offering access free of charge to more than 650,000 full-text articles, journals, books other resources. Its focus is on theology, intercultural and interreligious dialogue, ethics, and ecumenism in World Christianity." African Theology Worldwide, "Global Digital Library."

24. Regnum Books is one such example.

25. Ewell is currently executive director, WEA Theological Commission.

26. Julie Ma, personal diary.

and personal websites that regularly publish studies. Such publishing media have added functions such as audio and video material to augment the texts and interactive conversation between authors and readers. Search capability also adds convenience to traditional books. Another ground-breaking feature of electronic publishing is shareability, as seen by the growing number of portals providing related content. Additionally, online libraries are now more accessible and contain a wealth of studies that would be difficult to disseminate in other ways. Established Western publishers and many non-Western authors increasingly publish their works on new and traditional channels. Non-Western authors are even given preference by some publishers. Simultaneously, many Latin American, African, Asian, and Eastern European publishers are creating top-notch research for a worldwide audience.[27]

Editing, therefore, may offer a unique means of enabling young people from the Global South to collaborate with esteemed Western scholars on the same co-edited book. The editor creates a new space where scholars worldwide can work together. During the process, participants receive empowerment from the Lord and one another; they also gain a deeper understanding of the subject and discover new contexts to apply their research, such as South-to-North and South-to-South exchanges. Several academic journal editors promote these exchanges by including up-and-coming Global South researchers' perspectives. An example is Allan Anderson, a professor on Pentecostalism at Birmingham University in England, and I were co-authors of the article on Pentecostalism[28] in *Atlas of Global Christianity*, which provides more details in a footnote.

Conferences

Another way to share created knowledge is through professional conferences. Although this form shares several key common elements with

27. For example, "Globethics is an international non-governmental organisation, in consultative status with UN ECOSOC, dedicated to advancing ethical leadership worldwide. Building on 20 years of expertise and global trust, Globethics leverages its international network and strategic Geneva location to support the civil society, international organisations, private and public sectors in developing solutions to ethical dilemmas—moving beyond compliance towards impactful, values-driven governance and action across areas including technology, peacebuilding, higher education, and business." Globethics, "About Us."

28. Ma and Anderson, "Pentecostals," 100–101.

publishing, conferences provide live interaction. My first invitation for a paper presentation came right after my PhD graduation in June 1996 at the conference on "Pentecostalism in Globalization" in Costa Rica.[29] This opportunity came through a close friend who was mindful of encouraging our (my husband's) participation. When I saw the conference program flyer, I noticed some conference speakers were world-renowned scholars. It took much courage to stand before them, primarily because of my lack of experience. Since then, I have participated in various gatherings, often through invitations.[30]

Increased exposure leads to better recognition, increasing opportunities to participate and often share my studies in academic meetings and conferences. Through this experience, I have learned to take criticism from people. It is a natural human tendency that criticism discourages and intimidates; yet, through the years, I also began to learn not only to accept but also to appreciate various views and approaches that may differ from mine. Of course, we are encouraged through affirmation.

There are opportunities to meet and interact with many scholars in such spaces. I quickly learned that networking with creative and reflective minds benefited me and the institution I served. The most valuable experience in a conference is "getting to know" diverse groups with incredibly rich national and church orientations. I met the Japanese mission scholar Eiko Takamizawa, one of the paper presenters[31] at the International Symposium on Asian Mission in Manila held in January 2002. Another Asian woman scholar who contributed a paper at the Symposium was Melba P. Maggay.[32] Hearing what they said based on their experiences in their respective vocations has further enriched me. It is also an opportunity to share my unique expertise, which brings me a global dimension.

In 2005, I attended the Conference of World Mission and Evangelism of the World Council of Churches in Athens, Greece. Around eight hundred participants and staff from many churches and mission organizations were represented. This conference, like many others, opened me to new

29. "Pentecostalism in Globalization"; the conference was held in San Jose, Costa Rica.

30. Julie Ma, personal diary.

31. Takamizawa presented the paper on "A Model for Presenting the Gospel to Pantheists."

32. Melba P. Maggay is a Filipino social anthropologist who is director, Institute for Studies in Asian Church and Culture (ISACC), Manila, Philippines. Maggay presented on "Early Protestant Missionary Efforts in the Philippines: Some Intercultural Issues."

experiences. The house group of six to eight people came daily for devotion (called *lectio divina*) and reflection. The slow and repeated reading of a passage brought me deeper into communion with God and with the others. Equally valuable was the variety of worship presentations by different church traditions. Orthodox worship, for example, was highly liturgical, whereas Pentecostal worship was extremely spontaneous. Such dynamic experiences helped me embrace differences rather than fear them.

There are, of course, many formidable challenges, especially for a woman theologian like me. Financial resources always need help. Fatigue from frequent travels is another, and how to balance this commitment with teaching duties can be a severe issue. It is also possible that such opportunities do not come our way. My advice for the last one is to accept the first invitation. If still no opportunities arise, create one in the school or church where one serves. The first step is always challenging, and this is where a mentor's role is critical. Established Western colleagues can play an important role. My fundamental challenge as an Asian woman theologian is to be a good steward of my training and opportunities while increasing my God-given gift of knowledge to contribute toward his kingdom. One of the Pentecostals' favorite quotations, and mine, is Mark 9:23, "Everything is possible for him who believes."

Female Decision-Makers: The Unresolved Challenge

Despite all the contributions Asian women have made to Christianity worldwide, it is still unclear how much work they have done in the national governing bodies of Pentecostal organizations. Members of the national mission committee, district-level administrators, and high denominational officers are examples of these roles. At the federal level, women do not always occupy many leadership roles; males do. However, the dearth of females occupying these roles indicates a glass ceiling for their leadership ascent. My participation in the 2000 Edinburgh Centenary Celebration was distinct. There were twelve council members and six executive members, including me. I had a significant role in making decisions. Most women only stay involved in ministry at the local church, in missionary work, or in education.

Paul was quite fond of Priscilla and Aquila in Corinth. Even while the church organization had not yet reached a certain level of sophistication, Priscilla's role was most definitely that of a leader in her local congregation and leadership growth. Priscilla and Aquila assisted Paul in founding churches in Ephesus and Rome. He listed them as some of his most dependable colleagues and gave them high marks for their leadership qualities. Paul listened to their suggestions and respected their viewpoints (Acts 18:18–19, 24–26; Rom 16:3–5; 1 Cor 16:19; and 2 Tim 4:19).

Women can contribute considerably to church and denominational decision-making through solid attention to detail and relational sensitivity. Given their political position and accomplishments, how crucial is it for women to have more agency and influence in the church?

As I wrap up our discussion of Asian women's contributions to global Christianity, I want to raise this vital query: What would it take for Asian Pentecostal churches and denominations to elect or name women to positions of leadership within their denomination, such as heads of departments? It is uncommon to find a female denominational head among Pentecostal congregations. A recent surprise was the election of a female general superintendent by the Mongolian Assemblies of God, a new Pentecostal church. Yet, these exceptions highlight that males continue to hold the highest positions in these ecclesial organizations. The glass ceiling is still in place as a result.

CONCLUDING REMARKS

Women in the Global South are called to make severe contributions to the Christian mission. Their potential is often buried in culturally hostile environments. Therefore, men and women must be keenly aware of God-given gifts and opportunities. Often, women themselves need to be assured of their hidden and abundant potential, which they can cultivate and use for Christian missions on a global level. It will also take hard work and preparation while promoting a conducive environment. In many places in the Global South, women devalue themselves under the pretense of humility. Although I shared my own story, I never thought of myself as being an exceptionally qualified person. My family even disowned me for my Christian faith. As a daughter of my context, I had to constantly fight cultural norms and values with the liberating message of the gospel. However, I still must be conscious of my upbringing, which includes distorted values on human sexuality, as a part of myself.

The seismic shift of global Christianity and rapid changes in various cultures and social systems open new possibilities for men and women.

There are new opportunities for women in the Global South to play a critical role in shaping a new global Christianity. What are these implications? If the churches in the South are going to become active missionary churches, it will take women to assess their callings and gifts seriously. If women and children are often disadvantaged in education, health, and social opportunities, women must be significantly empowered by the gospel and the church. This is where a severe call is issued to a few women who have obtained higher education while deeply involved in the mission. I was able to sample only a tiny area of possibilities for them. Those women, particularly in academic circles, must continue their mission engagement to remain reflective practitioners and produce material that will impact the future of global Christianity and its mission. If one says we are not yet ready, we can start now to prepare for the future of the global church. Now, there is still time.

2

Korean Pentecostal Spirituality

A Case Study of Jashil Choi

Most sincere Korean believers are carrying out a constant prayer life. Some of them leave their daily routine, find a secluded place, and have a period of prayer and fasting for occasions or the solution of serious problems. As a sharer of this spiritual tradition, I know that the spirituality of Korean Pentecostals would never be complete once prayer and fasting were removed. They are two key components to building spirituality and successful church work. Prayer is a direct communication to and with a Divine Being, through which one can keep one's spiritual life and obtain spiritual power to do God's work. If prayer is coupled with fasting, it intensifies one's spiritual life. An individual's spirituality, especially church leaders, directly affects community ministry.

Jashil Choi epitomized such spirituality among Korean Pentecostals. I met her in the early years of my missionary life. In 1983, the third year of our lives in the Philippines, Yonggi Cho held a mass public crusade in Manila. Korean residents, students, and missionaries enthusiastically participated in the event. Jashil Choi, Cho's mother-in-law, invited several Korean ministers to her hotel room on the second day. I had not met her until then. She warmly welcomed us and asked us to lay hands on her twisted ankle for complete healing. She held my hand and comforted me at some point as if she had known me for many years. She even handed me a substantial offering for my struggling missionary family. Such a fond memory swelled immediately when I was reading her autobiography.

This chapter thoroughly delineates her spirituality reflected in her life of prayer and fasting and its effect on her ministry, mainly through the Yoido Full Gospel Church (YFGC) and the Choi Jashil International Fasting and Prayer Mountain (CJIFPM). While reading the book, I was often awestruck by extraordinary accounts of her life. Choi's life consisted of fasting and prayer, often through the night. Each challenging moment of her life and ministry was overcome through her fervent prayer. Having experienced the power of prayer, she was determined to establish a prayer mountain with a distinct emphasis on fasting despite the strong opposition of some church leaders. Her determination was so strong that even Cho could not stand in her way despite unfavorable circumstances.

The evidence of her spirituality was felt strongly from the pioneering year of the YFGC, originally called Full Gospel Central Church, to its growth as the world's largest church. Undoubtedly, Yonggi Cho's spiritual leadership single-handedly influenced the development of the church. Still, he frequently acknowledged the critical role of Choi's sacrificial prayer with fasting in the growth and development of the ministry: "Pastor Choi, my mother-in-law, is the person whom I would never forget in my life. If she were not my pastoral companion, I would not be a pastor in the world's largest church."[1] He sincerely admitted Choi's powerful spiritual and ministerial effect on his ministry. Her spirituality shows her deep spiritual commitment to the Lord and a case of creative contextualization of the Korean Pentecostal faith.

WHAT IS SPIRITUALITY?

There are many ways to define spirituality. It can be broad or narrow depending on how one comprehends its content. Perhaps a traditional approach to spirituality focuses on seeking the presence of God in prayer, meditation, contemplation, and fasting to learn God's heart and desire and adopt his character. This spiritual life is desirous to carry on into a solid pattern of Christian living. It is furthermore encouraged to be put into practice to generate the fruit of the Spirit: "love, joy, peace, patience, kindness . . ." (Gal 5:22–23). It takes some time to bear fruit in one's Christian life. A tree never bears a single fruit immediately. This implies that spiritual formation

1. Cho expressed it in the preface of Choi, *I Was Mrs. Hallelujah.*

does not occur in a split-second but may be a life-long process. Spirituality will make life worth living and produce a valuable life by reflecting its maturity.

A great Christian thinker, C. S. Lewis, exerted to form his spiritual life through self-giving: giving one's whole self to Christ, all personal wishes and precautions. Instead of being self-centered, focusing on worldly pleasure or ambition, one must be honest and humble to conform to sound doctrines, such as giving up self-desire. Lewis contemplates seriously how one can keep such a valuable life. He expresses that "a thistle cannot produce figs." "I cannot produce wheat if I am a field that contains nothing but grass seed. Cutting the grass may keep it short, but I shall still produce grass and no wheat. The change must go deeper than the surface if I want to produce wheat. I must be plowed up and resown."[2] Lewis is aware of the value of being selfless, which shows his spiritual maturity.

Born in North Africa, St. Augustine lived in a monastic community for thirty-four years and confessed his struggle to build spirituality. He has been considered one of the most significant thinkers in the history of the Christian church. Augustine's spirituality focuses on an ongoing debate about surrendering to the will of Christ, through which he believed he could get into deep faith. He desired to live according to the will of God, but he could not fully conform to it, thus he agonized under such a growing process. He gave an interesting analogy that the mind gives a direction to the body and is obeyed at certain times, but when it gives an order to itself, it is not accepted. In other words, when the mind orders the mind to structure an act of will, the order is not obeyed. He further argued that when the mind commands itself to fulfill an act of will, it will not give this order unless it is willing to do so. The command is not obeyed because it is not conferred with brimful will.[3] As Paul cried out over the struggle of the law of Spirit and body (Rom 7:14–25), Augustine likewise experienced the same dilemma. His sole desire was to fully conform to the will of God and live according to Christ's will for him. Here, the will most likely contains all biblical teachings and follows the promise of Christ, thus living an authentic spiritual life.

Then, how do Pentecostals understand spirituality? Russell Spittler, noted for his interest in the subject, consents that spirituality consists of behaviors and contemplation learned by the beliefs and values that identify

2. Lewis, "Excerpts from Mere Christianity," 31–32.

3. St. Augustine, "Confessions" 52–58.

a particular religious fellowship.[4] Spittler presents five specific values ruling Pentecostal spirituality.[5] Firstly, it refers to personal experience in accomplishing religious contentment. Personal experience, especially for Pentecostals, is truly guided by the presence of the Holy Spirit. They desire to know more about God through a spiritual journey. Secondly, orality.[6] For Pentecostals, it is vital to express what the Divine Being has accomplished in their lives through his love, goodness, faithfulness, and mercifulness. The affective dimension, which is eminently developed, would be demonstrated orally for Pentecostals. Thus, Pentecostals value orality as high as the written record regarding sharing their empirical experience with Jesus Christ. Thirdly, spontaneity is counted as Pentecostal devoutness. Spirituality is being exercised in intensity during worship time. It is because the Holy Spirit came upon those worshipers who waited on and welcomed the Spirit to lead. Thus, Pentecostals cannot keep themselves in silence. Fourthly, the notion of otherworldliness is firmly embedded in their spiritual life. The actual world is not visible; it is the invisible and eternal world. Such perception prevails more at the grassroots level than in the upper-middle class.

I have noticed that tribal people in northern Luzon[7] are fond of songs containing ideas of "hope" and "heaven" or songs of the Second Coming. Their dire living conditions cause them to draw closer to the Savior and to increase their hope in the eternal world. Lastly, making allegiance to biblical authority is one of the Pentecostal spiritual characteristics. Their high consideration for biblical authority and diligent learning to take the message of the scriptures at face value are shared among the Pentecostals.[8] Balancing both beliefs and practices is of significant value that Pentecostals highly regard. Thus, Pentecostal spirituality is not transcendental or philosophical but practical and tangible, and such spirituality facilitates the encounter of God in a unique way.

4. Spittler, "Spirituality," 804.

5. Spittler, "Spirituality," 804–5.

6. Hollenweger, "Pentecostal Research," vii–ix.

7. There are twelve major tribes and many unknown tribes within six provinces in the mountains of the northern Philippines. Pentecostal churches among the grass-root animistic tribal group of people were established through intensive power manifestation around 1947.

8. Spittler, "Spirituality," 805.

CHOI'S PERSONAL BACKGROUND

Choi was born in 1915 in Haeju City in Hwang-hae Province of North Korea during the Japanese occupation. When she was still young, her father died. After that, she had to take up a heavy responsibility and assist her mother, who made a tiny income from her sewing job. At the age of twelve, she and her mother had a chance to attend a tent revival meeting led by Sung-Bong Lee, a well-known Holiness preacher in early Korean Christian history. During this meeting, they accepted Christ as their personal Savior. Their great desire was to overcome poverty and become rich. Choi entered a nursing school to become a nurse and worked as a midwife to achieve this goal. Nurses earn good money while enjoying a decent life and respect. Choi's diligence and hard work led her close to the goal. She married an affluent and educated man.[9]

After moving to Seoul, South Korea, from the north, she opened a successful business. However, the more money she made, the emptier her heart became. And yet, she refused to go to church. Then a tragedy befell her: her mother and the oldest daughter died about a ten-day interval from each other. That incident shook Choi so severely that she developed complex illnesses. She interpreted it as a penalization from God for her ambition, worldly desire, and life away from him. Coincidentally, her business went down miserably. In 1956, she attempted to kill herself as she was losing her hope to live.[10]

During this desperate period, she turned to the Lord. She headed to a prayer mountain where a famous revival speaker, Sung-Bong Lee, was conducting a revival meeting. There, she came back to the Lord. Lee's message strongly ministered to her heart and helped her open to the Holy Spirit. During prayer time, she experienced fire running through her body from above, and her tongue became twisted, and she spoke in a strange language. The Holy Spirit baptized her. She had a genuine encounter with the Lord and committed to him. She entered the Full Gospel Bible College to prepare for her future ministry.[11]

9. Choi, *I Was Mrs. Hallelujah*, 1–2.
10. Choi, *I Was Mrs. Hallelujah*, 4–5.
11. Choi, *I Was Mrs. Hallelujah*, 8–9.

PRAYER AND FASTING IN CHOI'S LIFE

The spirituality of Choi's life can be deduced from two key components: prayer and fasting. This spiritual practice has been long recognized as vital in a Christian life. According to Roberta C. Bondi, prayer is the fundamental reality in Christian lives. Prayer actualizes believers as they discover their focus on God.[12] Prayer leads God's people into growth, knowledge of, and a deepening love for God. E. M. Bounds notes that prayer must be the basis of Christian character, life, and living. This is Christ's law of prayer, forming it into the very being of the Christian. It should be the primary step and breath.[13] Thus, "prayer is the Christian's vital breath, the Christian's native air. His watchword at the gates of death; he enters heaven with prayer."[14]

Choi, in her book *How to Pray for Answer*,[15] illustrates the power of prayer found in Exod 17:8–16. Israel's war against the invading Amalekites at Rephidim depended entirely on Moses' praying hands. If he continually held up his hands, victory was on the Israelites, but the enemy won when his hands came down. Moses had to sit on a stone to win the battle while his assistants held Moses' hands. Choi emphasizes the importance of unceasing prayer, particularly amid difficulties in life.

Choi's prayer life was shaped during her Bible school years. In a sense, her life could have been exciting to be a student in her old age, but it was not. She had many responsibilities, including leaving her children in someone else's care and supporting them. Such a difficult situation drew her closer to God, and her spirituality in prayer developed. Choi constantly prayed during the designated hours she set up. She recalled the time when Yonggi Cho was ill with tuberculosis during the Bible school days. While no one paid any attention to or cared for him, she showed affection toward him with intense prayer for his healing.[16] Perhaps this incident encouraged them to cultivate a close relationship with each other. Her spirituality was not confined to her private life but was often demonstrated in her ministry life. Such a display of concern for people was part of her spiritual exercise. Choi fasted as often as her spirit was led. She believed fasting could draw

12. Choi, *I Was Mrs. Hallelujah*, 10.
13. Bounds, *Complete Works of E. M. Bounds on Prayer*, 247.
14. Bondi, *To Pray and to Love*, 247.
15. Choi, *How to Pray for Answer*, 144–52.
16. Choi, *I Was Mrs. Hallelujah*, 147–52.

one closer to the divine presence and enable one to offer more powerful prayers. As a result, problems were solved rather quickly through intense prayer and fasting, which helped develop personal benefits.

Arthur Wallis believes that spirituality is exercised through fasting for the enduement of power, for spiritual gifts for physical healing, and for specific answers to prayer.[17] Choi also argued similarly on the prominence of fasting. This discovery was made through her long and deeply spiritual journey. Her desire for a sound spiritual life through prayer and fasting led her to establish a prayer mountain dedicated to fasting. Long and intensive prayer with frequent fasting naturally characterized this process. The more time she spent in prayer and fasting, the stronger her faith became for the first prayer mountain with a distinct emphasis on fasting.

In the meantime, she began to search for a good location for prayer facilities. While praying and fasting, one night, she heard the voice of God directing her to a parcel of land for the prayer mountain. The place had been a cemetery for many years, and she might have felt a strong reluctance to bring it to the board. However, when she made an immediate visit to the place called Osan-ri village, she knelt on her knees on the barren ground surrounded by graves and prayed. After her daily ministry in the fast-growing church pastored by Yonggi Cho, she alone came to the cemetery and spent hours in prayer every night.[18] A woman with no company praying in the desolate field must have been a strange sight. It demonstrated her unreserved trust in God's promise and commitment to him. These short accounts of her early life and ministry will illustrate her unique spiritual life.

EFFECT OF CHOI'S SPIRITUALITY TO HER MINISTRY

Personal Evangelism

Choi had a marvelous heart for serving lost souls. She always availed herself to be used for the work of God's kingdom. During her training in the Bible school, she took every opportunity to bring the unsaved to Christ. Donald Whitney points out that evangelism is an intrinsic overflow of the Christian life. It is also the call of a disciple that all Christians follow the Lord in obedience and evangelism. Therefore, each Christian must actively

17. Wallis, *God's Chosen Fast*, 55–59.

18. Choi, *I Was Mrs. Hallelujah*, 29–33.

witness rather than wait for a moment to come.[19] Matthew 5:16 fits well this context: "Let your light shine before men, that they may see your good deeds and praise your Father in heaven." Whitney correctly interprets that to "let" the light shine before others means more than "don't do anything to keep your light from shining." The closest rendering is: "Let the light of good works shine in your life, the evidence of God-honoring change radiating from you. Let it begin! Make room for it!"[20] Choi's unique strategy was to approach children for evangelism. Choi had a natural ability to draw children to her. Even in evangelism, prayer was the bedrock of her ministry. She spent more time on prayer and fasting than in actual evangelism.

In 1957, Choi graduated from the Bible College but was unsure about her future ministry. For her to discover God's direction, she fervently prayed with fasting for many days. At one point, Choi seriously considered operating an orphanage since she had a heart for children, but she soon learned that it was not God's best intention for her. Nonetheless, Choi continually exerted herself for children's evangelism. Her autobiography includes many incidents that illustrate her love for children's souls. Every night, her intense prayer included children.[21]

She gradually expanded her evangelistic activity for adults. Choi already had about seventy people in the fellowship each Sunday, plus many children. There was no suitable place to meet, so their gathering often occurred under a pine tree. Thus, rainy days posed extreme challenges. Once, in her regular prayer time in a quiet place, she heard the voice of God instructing her to start a tent church. "Hearing God's voice" was a regular part of her prayer life.

The Bible provides many cases where people spent time listening to God. First Kings 19:11–13 notes Elijah's effort to hear the gentle voice of God in a segregated Mount Horeb. Habakkuk (2:1) also stood on the guard post and kept attention to see or hear what God would speak to him. The depth of Choi's faith and trust was almost comparable with those of Bible characters, particularly in her desire and endurance to hear the divine voice. Bounds contends that trust and faith become absolute, validated, and accomplished in prayer. Trust is solid belief and faith in "full flower." It is an alert act, a fact to which believers are sensitive. According to the biblical notion, it is the eye of the infant soul and the ear of the regenerated soul.

19. Whitney, *Spiritual Disciples for the Christian Life*, 100.

20. Whitney, *Spiritual Disciples for the Christian Life*, 100.

21. Choi, *I Was Mrs. Hallelujah*, 213.

Such belief brings no wakefulness of their presence, no "joy unspeakable and full of glory" results from their exertion.[22] Christ showed that trust is the foundation of prayer. The central issue of Christ's ministry and work was his faith in his Father. When trust is complete, prayer is simply an outstretched hand ready to receive.[23] Trust always operates not in the past but in the present tense.

With God's assurance, Choi immediately rushed to a tent store to purchase one. A tent in those days was not inexpensive. Even though the tent was not of good quality, with joy bubbling, the tent was pitched on the outskirts of Seoul, surrounded by makeshift houses and graves. Her zeal for soul-winning increased, and many were added to the kingdom.

Sensitivity to Felt Needs

Choi found herself frequently caring for the needy and sick. Residents around the church were extremely poor; many were physically ill, and some neighbors were demon-possessed. One day, a poor family invited her to visit their mother, who had significantly been suffering for seven years with a severe case of paralysis. To make her situation worse, the mother had given birth recently and was not able to afford to buy nutritious food for recuperation. As a result, she was very sick. When Choi entered the room, a strong odor caused her nausea, and she almost threw up. She immediately prayed to overcome the difficult smell and embraced the family with love. The Lord spoke into her heart, "Do not just ask for love; get water and wash her body."[24] Upon hearing the voice of God, Choi washed the malodorous body of the woman and even her children.

Her deep spirituality is a tangible embodiment of what Abba Poemen stated:

> There is nothing greater in love than that a [person] lay down [that person's] life for his [or her] neighbor. When a [person] hears a complaining word and struggles against himself [or herself] and does not . . . begin to complain; when a [person] bears an injury with patience and does not look for revenge; that is when a [person] lays down his [or her] life for his [or her] neighbors.[25]

22. Bounds, *Complete Works of E. M. Bounds on Prayer*, 24.
23. Bounds, *Complete Works of E. M. Bounds on Prayer*, 26.
24. Choi, *I Was Mrs. Hallelujah*, 227.
25. Bondi, *To Pray and to Love*, 112.

Bondi characterizes God's love not as the love of disinterest and that of a king for his aloof subjects; it is close, tender, and defenseless, as a mother's is for her child.[26] Choi's action revealed the genuine love of God toward her neighbor in an extreme need. Choi often cried with pain in her heart for this family. She constantly visited them and compassionately offered deep prayers for their healing and conversion. The family's situation was worsened by the heavy drinking of the husband day and night, who never paid any attention to the family. Even with her own financial difficulty, Choi bought bread and rice for the family.[27] She understood how God treats the poor: "Has not God chosen those who are poor in the eyes of the world to be rich in faith and to inherit the kingdom" (Jas 2:5). Verse 6 continues, "But you have insulted the poor." Matthew records the attitude of the Lord: "If you want to be perfect, go, sell your possessions and give to the poor, and you will have treasure in heaven" (Matt 9:21).

Similarly, George Soares Prabhu argues that to be a follower of Christ means experiencing God the way that Jesus had experienced God. One essential element for Christian self-definition is the experience of God's love, which encourages us to love in effectual compassion to those in want.[28] The poor are indeed the object of God's concern and care. Appropriately appropriating God's compassion toward the needy is essential to Christian spirituality. Choi's spirituality is a good example. It was expressed in cleaning smelly rooms and bathing children regularly. In addition, she once fasted for three days for the mother's healing and the entire family's salvation. She constantly read the Bible and prayed to encourage their faith. Through her persevering prayer, the paralytic woman began to rise and take fragile steps. Tremendous divine power was manifested fifteen days later when the woman could get up and work for the family. Such events caused others to open their eyes and come to the Lord.

Choi was assured of the power of fasting in supplication for healing. She expounded on the prominence of fasting in prayer in her book *How to Pray for Answer*, drawing examples from the scriptures.[29] Hezekiah was her outstanding example. He was a spiritual man who put total trust in the Lord for the peace of the nation (2 Kgs 18:6). When he was fatally ill and

26. Bondi, *To Pray and to Love*, 29.
27. Choi, *I Was Mrs. Hallelujah*, 232–33.
28. Prabhu, "Jesus of Faith," 18.
29. Choi, *How to Pray for Answer*, 315–16.

about to die, he wept bitterly to God for healing. His supplication resulted in divine grace, expanding his life by fifteen more years.

Spiritual Warfare

Throughout her ministry, Choi encountered many demon possession cases. After a Sunday worship service, a member from a neighboring church rushed to her, asking Choi to visit her friend whom a terrible sickness had tormented. The sick woman was not a Christian, and she was always referred to shamans for healing and advice. One day, the shaman gave a striking "revelation": if she failed to become a shaman through a special ritual, she would die soon. Upon hearing such a dreadful verdict, her family fiercely opposed the idea. Out of great anxiety, she shared her problem with her Christian friend.[30] It proves that Choi was quite well known in the area as a woman filled with the Spirit as she earnestly desired to minister to people who were going through difficulties.

Bounds notes that religion has to do with everything but our hearts. It requires our hands and feet to give full devotion. It takes hold of our voices to praise. It lays its hands on our material concerns and does not only take hold of personal affections, desires, and enthusiasm.[31] One may add that our sincere heart is not only for worship and praise but also to serve with our hands and feet, laying down human selfishness and fervor.

Choi and her ministry partner, Yonggi Cho, were brought to the sick woman's house. She suddenly sat down when they entered the room and stared at them like an angry rooster. Choi and the accompanying members quietly sat on the floor and began to sing hymns. Choi instantaneously knew that Satan attempted to attack.[32] Ephesians 6:10–20 states such a spiritual struggle. Believers are caught in the idea of eschatological tension that is "already, but not yet." Apostle Paul was aware of two different realms of power: God and the devil. It is also apparent that the world as the dominion of darkness is on one side, while Christ, Christians, and the power and authority of God are on the other.[33] With this understanding, Choi and her group sang continually and rebuked the evil spirit in the woman with the authority of Christ. In the middle of singing and prayer, the woman

30. Choi, *I Was Mrs. Hallelujah*, 315–16.

31. Bounds, *Complete Works of E. M. Bounds on Prayer*, 92.

32. Choi, *I Was Mrs. Hallelujah*, 317.

33. Arnold, *Ephesians*, 156–57.

abruptly uttered in Japanese, "Let's go. Let's go to Japan." (Choi spoke and understood Japanese like many Koreans who lived during the Japanese occupation.) Then, the woman seemed to be back to normal.

The Japanese language was spoken not by the woman but by Satan. According to the woman, she went to Japan to study as a young girl and stayed there for several years. During this period, she became a member of a religious group. Then, she returned to Korea and married a man. When she was pregnant with her first child, she was ill, and the sickness continued until Choi's ministry. Through the power of God displayed in prayer, the woman was delivered from her bondage. Such manifestation of God's power led her entire family and relatives to the Lord. Power encounter is a regular part of Christian spiritual life, especially among Pentecostals. Thus, the concept has been used among Asian Christians without question. However, some believers feel reluctant to use such a term because of its military connotation. Alan Tippett first used this term to refer to a conflict between the kingdom of God and Satan.[34] It frequently occurs, especially among tribal groups who believe in the spiritual world and the involvement of the spirits in their life. During the ministry of Jesus, he drove out many demons from people. The demonstration of God's power was also frequent in the Old Testament. One of the outstanding instances is the story of Elijah, confronting the four hundred and fifty prophets of Baal on Mount Carmel (1 Kgs 18:16–45). Oscar Cullmann notes that Satan still has great power, the power that can destroy any human being and his or her plan if they remain without encumbrance.[35] Thus, divine power and authority are essential for effective work in God's kingdom. John Wimber argues that unity also facilitates the believers to experience God's power.[36] In the book of Acts, when believers came together in one accord, the power of God was manifested. It is noted that Choi's spiritual exercise with prayer and fasting played a significant role in her successful evangelistic ministry.

Establishment of the Prayer Mountain

The church she had pioneered with Yonggi Cho on the outskirts of Seoul moved to town to accommodate the growing members. After the move, the membership grew to eighteen thousand, which continued for the next

34. Tippett, *People Movements in Southern Polynesia*, 81.

35. Cullmann, *Christ and Time*, 64.

36. Wimber and Springer, *Power Evangelism*, 58.

seven years. Cho was perfectly complemented by Choi's spiritual insights and gifts for these exceptional years of church growth. The church became particularly known for its healing ministry. When the church held a tent revival meeting with missionary Sam Todd, about two hundred people received healing.[37] As the church constantly grew in number, Cho and the church began to search for another location for a new church building. When Yoido Island was suggested, the odds were against Cho. First, Yoido was too far from the city center, and the future of the deserted military airfield was uncertain. This challenge took Choi frequently to a prayer mountain near Seoul. While she was imploring God for the church's future, the idea of starting a prayer mountain for the church suddenly entered her mind. She immediately noticed that it was not merely a human thought but was from God. With this assurance, Choi prayed every day for God's direction. In addition to the huge financial needs, the timing seemed wrong: the church was preparing for a huge, new facility. However, Choi did not abandon the vision. The vision grew stronger through her prayer. Every night, she went to the cemetery in Osan-ri and spent her time praying. Through the prayer mountain ministry, she wanted to bring the people of God to prayer life.[38] Yonggi Cho more than once underscored the importance of prayer: "We Koreans have made prayer our priority. From prayer has come communion and fellowship with the Holy Spirit. Today, the Holy Spirit guides us daily, and we have power with God through prayer."[39] Bondi had a holistic view of prayer: the possibilities of prayer influence all things. Whatever deals with people's highest well-being, and whatever has to do with God's scheme and will concerning human beings on earth is a subject for prayer. Prayer opens doors for access to the gospel.[40]

In addition to the financial challenge, some leaders of the church questioned the choice of the location. First, it was in the northern part, which was too close to the border with North Korea. In case of a North Korean invasion, the area could be devastated instantly. Secondly, there was no running water or trees, only graves. Such negative feedback caused Choi to feel that the prayer mountain was no longer possible, and she was despondent. Once, she prayed through the day and the whole night with some church members, and during her prayer, God gave her scriptures that

37. Choi, *I Was Mrs. Hallelujah*, 415–32.

38. Cho, "Prayer Can Change the Course of Your Life," 11.

39. Bondi, *To Pray and to Love*, 163.

40. Choi, *I Was Mrs. Hallelujah*, 432–33.

uplifted her enormously: John 14:1, "Do not let your hearts be troubled. Trust in God; trust also in me." Also, Phil 2:13–14 was another passage: "For it is God who works in you to will and to act according to his good purpose. Do everything without complaining or arguing." From these verses, Choi was assured that God would accomplish this vision through her.[41] It is relatively common among Pentecostals to expect the "leading of the Spirit": Pentecostals have a sense of hearing what the Spirit is speaking to them through the word of God and a personal encounter with God. The Lord showed a clear sign of his will: People from different places flocked into Osan-ri, which had not yet been purchased and was still barren. Those people who came prayed with fasting, and this became a rule for this prayer mountain. Soon, this place began to attract people from Japan and other parts of the world, and they discovered a new spiritual dimension through prayer and fasting. The Osan-ri Prayer Mountain became the first international facility for prayer and fasting. An increasing number of the sick came to experience divine healing. Soon, many experienced healings from incurable sicknesses through intensive and fervent prayer and fasting. Such news soon spread throughout the nation, and more people who were in desperate situations came to pray.

An emphasis on the power of prayer and fasting became the hallmark of Choi's spirituality. Joel 2:12 notes the significance of fasting: "Yet even now," says the LORD, "return to me with all your heart, with fasting." First Kings 21:27–29 also illustrates a similar point. After the murder of Naboth and Ahab's obligatory obtainment of his vineyard, God sent Elijah to declare divine judgment upon him. "When Ahab heard those words, he rent his clothes, put sackcloth upon his flesh, and fasted." God declared, "Because he has humbled himself before me, I will not bring evil in his days, but in his son's days." Judgment was postponed because even such an evil person as Ahab humbled himself by fasting. God's mercy is not limited to only righteous people but extends to anyone seeking God's mercy. Fasting displays how earnestly the people of God pray to him, especially in times of need. Arthur Wallis notes that fasting makes prayer ascend as on an eagle's wings. It is meant to usher the supplicant into the spectators' room of the Lord and to extend to him the golden scepter. It may be anticipated to drive back the oppressing powers of darkness and loosen their grip on the prayer

41. Wallis, *God's Chosen Fast*, 50.

objective. It is counted to give a brim to a man's intercessions and power to his petitions. The Lord is eager to listen when someone prays with fasting.[42]

Undoubtedly, fasting is an essential aspect of Christian life. Fasting is often an ultimate form of earnest and extended supplication. In the CJIFPM, initially called the Osan-ri Prayer Mountain, some fasted even for forty days. It is a spiritual wrestling between the supplicant and the Divine Being. Choi affirms that "fasting helps to express, to deepen, and to confirm the resolution that we are ready to sacrifice anything, to sacrifice ourselves to attain what we seek for the kingdom of God."[43]

Even though it was desolate, such testimonies and the increasing number of visitors to Osan-ri moved the hearts of church leaders to establish the prayer mountain. Ultimately, however, it was the Holy Spirit who accomplished the vision. During the early period of the prayer mountain, Choi fasted as frequently as three days a week. This exemplary prayer life has encouraged many to follow her example and has been drawn into profound spiritual experiences.

Choi's International Ministry

Choi's spiritual ministry soon crossed national boundaries and expanded to other countries. God opened a door for her to reach the Japanese, and church leaders repeatedly invited her. Before her preaching, Choi customarily spent a whole night in prayer for the next day's service. The effect of prayer was so evident that many people in the service were filled with the Holy Spirit. Also, a variety of manifestations of the Spirit took place regularly. Choi's anointed message, accompanied by the work of the Spirit, impacted many Japanese churches. Common themes of her message were repentance, prayer, and the Spirit-led life. When she visited a place, Choi eagerly ministered in as many churches as she could and offered a marvelous ministry. Her autobiography illustrates her eagerness as well. The Spirit was at work, particularly in healing, and often unprecedented miracles occurred. Soon, many people in Japan who were sick began to visit the prayer mountain in Osan-ri and spend days praying and fasting. Various spiritual gifts were manifested, including speaking in tongues and interpreting.

Many in the United States were called for ministry through her influence. Her ministry in Thailand, Hong Kong, Germany, and other places

42. Wallis, *God's Chosen Fast*, 50.

43. Choi, *I Was Mrs. Hallelujah*, 337–60.

produced similar results. Choi's international ministry was also her commitment to the missionary call found in Acts 1:8, "But you will receive power when the Holy Spirit comes on you; and you will be my witnesses in Jerusalem, and in all Judea and Samaria, and to the ends of the earth."[44] Before such trips, Choi spent two or three weeks in prayer and fasting. She was preparing for a forthcoming ministry and making herself a living message of God's power through prayer and fasting.

ASSESSMENT OF CHOI'S SPIRITUALITY

Her Influences on Korean Christianity

As discussed above, Choi's distinctive spirituality had substantial implications for her ministry: it was founded on prayer and fasting. Perhaps it is fair to say that such spirituality has been part of the spiritual tradition in various religions, particularly Korean Christianity. In the early revival in Pyongyang (1939), for instance, the three thousand members of Suemoon Church fasted while praying the whole night. The preacher was Jun Jasun, one of the great evangelists. Such an incident affected the members to encounter the power of the Holy Spirit, repentance, and spiritual renewal.[45] During the post-exilic period in the Old Testament, Jews commonly fasted as a form of prayer, and fasting became part of their spirituality. Even in New Testament times, Jews frequently fasted (Matt 6:16–18).

However, Choi's practice of prayer and fasting may not strictly be identified with the Jewish practice. As everyone would agree, prayer is essential to a Christian spiritual life. However, fasting requires additional commitment and effort. Perhaps an experience of fasting or two, especially in a desperate circumstance, could be possible without much severe discipline. However, fasting regularly as part of one's spiritual life was probably a new concept in Korean Christianity. From the beginning of her Christian life, fasting was crucial for cultivating her spiritual growth and developing an intimate relationship with the Lord. This also led her to broader and more profound spiritual experiences. For instance, before engaging in cases of demon possession, she fasted with fervent prayer, and she frequently experienced God's power to drive out the demon. Thus, one can acknowledge

44. International Theological Institutes, *History of the Korean Assemblies of God*, 183–84.

45. Preface of Choi, *I Was Mrs. Hallelujah.*

the importance of fasting in spiritual warfare. Fasting also enhanced many Christian works such as evangelism, preaching, missions, church growth, healing, and solving diverse problems. Her spiritual leadership and contribution through her intense prayer and fasting were an integral part of the unprecedented growth of the YFGC. Yonggi Cho acknowledged it openly, "if she were not my co-worker, I would not be able to accomplish such a successful pastoral ministry now."[46]

Challenges of Choi's Spirituality

Fasting and prayer have always been the main feature of Choi's spirituality. Her deep communion with God through prayer and fasting greatly heightened her sensitivity to the Spirit. Choi's unique spirituality, primarily through her prayer mountain ministry, set forth a new paradigm for Christian spirituality, and this became identified as Korean Pentecostal spirituality. Her teaching of prayer and fasting spread quickly to the entire Korean Christianity and beyond through the prayer mountain and the popular conferences she conducted in various countries. One such conference was in Jerusalem in October 1980. Around five hundred people came from different countries and had a four-day prayer rally with fasting. Thirty-four ministers from South Africa attended this conference and experienced a deep working of the Spirit. The participants learned how to pray with fasting, which became a significant part of their spiritual lives and churches. Consequently, fasting has become a standard or even an important spiritual/religious tradition across many countries. For example, I have seen an American fast for one day before he delivered a special lecture.

Her life-long devotion to, and campaign for, prayer and fasting changed the spiritual paradigm of the Korean church forever. Her life and ministry demonstrated that prayer is not just part of the Christian life, but prayer is the Christian life. When prayer is accompanied by fasting, the intensity of prayer is significantly enhanced. It is because fasting signifies a total surrender to God and a serious commitment to prayer. The example of Jesus shows this clearly in the Gospels. In the desert, he prepared himself for the messianic mission in prayer with forty-day fasting. After a long period of prayer, he returned to Galilee in the power of the Spirit. He was ready to launch his earthly mission (Luke 4:14). The unique spirituality of Choi is something that the people of God must adapt and apply to their

46. Allen, "Spirituality of the Psalms," 3.

spiritual life. Such spiritual exercise is perhaps more required in increasingly secularized modern societies so that the church can be the actual light in a darkened postmodern era.

CONCLUDING REMARKS

Choi's distinctive spirituality has been investigated in this chapter. Everywhere she went, her prayer life with fasting impacted practically millions of believers through her pastoral and international ministries. Subsequently, several more prayer mountains with particular emphasis on fasting were established, sometimes by herself but many others by people impacted by her ministry. Until her death, prayer, and fasting were the hallmarks of her life and ministry. I was amazed by her solid spiritual devotion, prayer with fasting, and how deeply it was laid in her life.

I received a tantamount challenge from her life of prayer and fasting. Fasting is challenging for me. I have done it occasionally, but that laborious exercise slowly disappeared from my spiritual life as the years went by. However, as I studied Choi's spirituality, I realized the significance of fasting. Consequently, prayer and fasting have slowly become a part of my spiritual journey.

Many believers whom Choi influenced were boldly involved in extensive fasting. In particular, members of the YFGC were well taught. Cell group heads and church leaders are taken to the CJIFPM on the first days of the new year to pray and fast. Regular bus trips leave the church often daily, going to the prayer mountain. I witnessed many rides on a bus and spent at least a night for the prayer right after the church service. Spirituality is the human response to God, prompted by theology's intersection with a believer's real life. An intense and continuous interaction between God and his children shaped Choi's life and ministry. Indeed, prayer is one of the most meaningful ways to experience the presence of God. Choi taught us how to have a more prosperous and profound experience through fasting. I pray that Choi's rich spiritual legacy and heritage will continue encouraging and challenging many believers to cultivate their spirituality through prayer and fasting. There is nothing more important in the Christian life than experiencing God himself regularly.

3

Impact of a Female Missionary in Igorot Mission, Northern Luzon, Philippines

In the early stage of the Assemblies of God mission movement (around 1900), the participation of female leadership was well accepted. It was essential in bringing a lively revival and moving mission work. Both single and married women were called and responded to various ministries, such as church planting, evangelization, nursing, and teaching, in the far-flung corners of the world. They were anointed for specific tasks, which was more important than human authorization.

In 1947, the Assemblies of God began ministry among the Kankanaeys, one of the Igorot tribal groups, in the Philippines.[1] The ministry was initiated by a single missionary woman from America and a few local leaders. The missionary, Elva Vanderbout, was commissioned by the Foreign Mission Department in Springfield, Missouri, in 1946.[2] Until she launched her work in the mountains, no missionaries or national workers of the Assemblies of God had attempted mountain ministry. Vanderbout approached this tribal group with a unique Christian message: God's power. Churches were established through the message of divine power and its manifestation, and the mountain ministry of the Assemblies of God was successfully carried on. This section will delineate her specific mission work in various contexts and further analyze and evaluate her ministry.

1. Jenks, *Igorot*, in English is "mountaineer" (i.e., "one who dwells in the mountain"). Scott further elaborates that from the archaic term *golot* (mountain chain) and the prefix "i" (dweller in or people from), *Igorot* carries the meaning "mountaineer." Scott, "Igorot Responses," 695–717.

2. Vanderbout, "Application for Appointment as Missionary."

THE CALL OF GOD TO ELVA VANDERBOUT

In 1944, a mission convention was held at the Bethel Temple church in Los Angeles, where Elva Vanderbout attended. One speaker was Howard Osgood, a missionary to China.[3] On the second morning of the convention, Vanderbout sat in front of the church auditorium. The song service immediately started; during this time, she felt a great sense of the brooding of the Holy Spirit. Mission songs spoke to her more personally and directly than she had ever experienced. When a speaker was sharing a message on the millions of people who were lost, idol worshipers, and those people who were in darkness and paganism, the message pointedly reached her. A speaker invited church members who wanted to give their lives for the lost to come forward. Her heart was broken as she sensed the presence of God. Vanderbout was one of the first to answer. She almost ran to the altar, put her hands up in total surrender, and prayed, "I give myself to You! I will do what You ask me to do! I will go where You ask me to go! Oh, God." Then she heard the voice of God, "Whom shall I send, and who will go for me?" From the depths of her heart, she was answering, "Here am I, send me . . . ." In the meantime, Vanderbout's husband was terribly ill due to a cerebral hemorrhage. The disease paralyzed the left side of his body, rendering him bedridden and in need of full attention. When her husband died, Vanderbout's heart was indeed broken.[4] Vanderbout turned her thoughts to where she should go a few months after the funeral. One day, the pastor's wife asked her if she had decided which country to go to for mission work. Mrs. Turnbull, the pastor's wife, mentioned the Philippines. Upon hearing the country's name, she loved thinking of going to the Philippines. Sometime later, a chance came to Vanderbout to contact a missionary couple from the Philippines. Vanderbout received the necessary information about the country from them and was excited about going to the Philippines as a missionary.[5] She was officially ordained to be a missionary in 1946 by the Foreign Missions Department in Springfield.[6]

December 15, 1946, Vanderbout left her land to reside in the Philippines. She traveled by ship to the Philippines via different countries. The ship was jammed with adults and children so she could hardly find a space

3. Sturgeon, *Give Me This Mountain*, 28.
4. Sturgeon, *Give Me This Mountain*, 36–47.
5. Sturgeon, *Give Me This Mountain*, 54.
6. Vanderbout, "Application for Appointment as Missionary" (1946).

to lean her body. Vanderbout felt unutterable weariness with the situation. She managed to find a tiny space on the third deck, which was the worst place.[7] However, she attempted to get through long days and nights with prayer. After twenty-three days of a long and tedious journey, the islands of the Philippines began to loom nearby. Vanderbout sparkled with joy at reaching the destination she had long been waiting for.

On January 7, 1947, Vanderbout finally trod the soil of the Philippine Islands to begin mission work. After a twelve-day stay in Manila, she left for Baguio City, where she would eventually start her ministry among these people.[8] The road was extremely rough as most bridges had been bombed during the war and had not yet been rebuilt, so the bus had to ford streams and gullies. At that time, the population of Baguio City was thirty thousand. Much of the city had been demolished during the war.[9] However, Vanderbout was gladly welcomed by the Assemblies of God church members. Vanderbout's clear call from God eventually directed her to the Philippines; it was apparent that God's hand was upon the specific decision path. The burden that Vanderbout had for the mountain people was endowed by God. God's divine intervention in her life was vivid and vital. Her desire to reach out to the mountain people was thus slowly coming to realization.

VANDERBOUT'S INITIAL MISSION WORK

In 1947, Vanderbout began her ministry in Tuding,[10] Itogon, notorious as a nest of criminal elements and the most wicked and sinful place in the mountain province after World War II. There were robberies, assaults, knifings, and police raids. About two thousand people lived in Tuding, and twenty-one thousand inhabitants lived in surrounding areas.[11] Vanderbout visited Tuding one night, wanting to know what sort of place it was. When she returned home that night, she could not erase from her mind the picture of the Tuding barrio, and she became so profoundly burdened for the people. National leaders advised her not to begin the ministry in such an evil place; it might endanger her life. But Vanderbout persisted and

7. Sturgeon, *Give Me This Mountain*, 69–75.

8. Sturgeon, *Give Me This Mountain*, 76–80.

9. Vanderbout, "Westward Move," 1.

10. Tuding is located in Benguet Province in Northern Luzon in the Philippines.

11. Vanderbout, "Westward Move," 1.

started her ministry in Tuding. Despite the peril she would encounter, she was assured that God had called her to these people. Vanderbout thus sincerely responded to the call of God and her commitment paralleled the call. Vanderbout wrestled with how to begin her ministry among these people for a few months. She spoke in the Baguio church, started Bible study classes, and conducted prayer meetings, but she wanted a stable ministry to win the souls in darkness. With much prayer and understanding that a woman would find it challenging to approach pagan people with a new religion, Vanderbout thought of children in a public elementary school in Tuding as a population among whom she could begin her ministry. That ministry became, for Vanderbout, a stepping stone to spreading the gospel among the mountain people. She visited Tuding Elementary School to meet the principal and to suggest her ideas. To her amazement, the principal permitted her to open a Bible class. It was marvelous for a single woman to get permission to minister in any local public school in the male-dominated mountain world. It was another apparent work of the Holy Spirit.[12] July 26, 1947, was her first day at the Tuding school. Vanderbout presented the gospel through the interpretation of local workers. She supplemented her words with exciting materials that fascinated the children; they had never seen such objects. The visual aids drew their rapt attention to the message of the gospel.[13]

Vanderbout continued her ministry among the children. Distinctively the fifth and sixth grades were the most interested in the gospel. The children comprehended the gospel quite well and responded heartwarmingly. Vanderbout's initial ministry among children was thus successful. The ministry became a foundation to spread the gospel further to the children's parents. As Vanderbout continued her ministry among these school children, some girls and boys wanted Vanderbout to visit their parents. Vanderbout prayed earnestly about visiting the homes of these girls and boys. The Holy Spirit told her that this was the door God had opened for her to reach these people. She made up her mind to accept invitations and visit the homes. She and her local workers, who assisted her in interpretation, hiked twelve miles to visit the children's homes. The parents responded positively to the gospel message; this was the first time they heard the word of God.[14]

12. Ma, *When the Spirit Meets the Spirits*, 76–77.

13. Ma, *When the Spirit Meets the Spirits*, 76.

14. Personal interview with Leoraldo Caput, Tuding, Benguet, Philippines, March 15, 1993.

One of Vanderbout's experiences with a sick person who was the father of one of her "students" resulted in bringing a whole family to God. When the missionary visited the girl's home, her father was paralyzed on his whole left side and had been on the floor for six months. Their living conditions were so poor that the patient had no blanket or pillow. This scene broke Vanderbout's heart, especially in retrospect of her husband's death. A burden to share the gospel welled up in Vanderbout's heart. Vanderbout regularly visited the paralyzed man and shared the living word of God. The whole family found the Lord as their Savior through her ministry to the sick man and earnestly sharing the message. After many such conversions, many of these parents became the pillars of the Tuding church.[15]

Vanderbout, even though she was a single female missionary, was well accepted by native Kankana-ey people because of her passion and love for these people. One advantage for Vanderbout, despite being a female, was that she was a white woman, and the mountain people tended to respect white women. Above all, the Holy Spirit intervened in her ministry to bring effectiveness.

PENTECOST IN TUDING

Vanderbout did not confine herself to children's ministry. She wanted to expand her work in Tuding, Itogon. She and her ministry team thus started evangelism in Tuding. Vanderbout soon found that each time they preached the gospel, more and more people were coming to hear the message of God. Vanderbout eventually decided to hold open-air services to accommodate the crowds. As she frequently met these people, she noticed many attendees were afflicted by disease. She learned that during the war, most of the mountain people lost all of their possessions, leaving them poverty-stricken and devastated. Poor living conditions caused them to lose bodily resistance to disease.[16]

The earliest converts among the Codilleran were Paran Bukayan and a few of his relatives. Bukayan opened his house for Sunday morning and evening services.[17] Bukayan had heard about the ministry and compassion of Vanderbout among the mountain people and had invited Vanderbout

15. Interview with Caput.

16. Sturgeon, *Give Me This Mountain*, 93.

17. Soriano, "Pentecost in the Philippines," 1, quoted in Vanderbout, "Personal Newsletter to the Foreign Mission Department."

to speak at a service. At this point, Vanderbout was well known among the village people in Tuding. News of Vanderbout's preaching in this service spread among the village people through Bukayan's relatives. Pagan people came to the service with an interest in what a white woman would attempt to speak. The message was powerfully delivered to people gathered, and many newcomers turned to Christ. The power of the Holy Spirit empowered the people attending. The good news of Christ began to work to change people's hearts. The congregation of the house church grew larger.

In 1948, Vanderbout and local ministers held revival meetings in Tuding week after week, besides having regular services on Sunday nights. The Holy Spirit moved among the gathered people. Many nonbelievers were saved, and more than 150 were baptized in water. The old, the young adults, and the children shared terrific testimonies of the power of God, which saved their lives from darkness and the bondage of sin. They rejoiced with salvation and became new creatures.[18] Every Sunday night service, many people were baptized with the Holy Ghost and fire, according to Acts 2:4. It was like old-time Pentecost. As the place for service was packed full every Sunday night, Vanderbout came to see the urgent need to build a church. What attracted the animists? It was God's power revealed so vividly through the message and prayer. The power they experienced differed from the power of ancestor spirits mediated by a pagan priest. Many received visions from the Lord and were called into God's service.[19]

A remarkable Pentecost was indicated in Vanderbout's newsletter sent to the Department of Foreign Missions of the Assemblies of God. It said:

> Two weeks ago, after a beautiful time of prayer, we were about to dismiss and go home when the power began to fall again, and a message in tongues came forth, and the LORD gave the interpretation. Everybody fell to their knees again and began to cry out to God. Many sinners were present who had just come in to see what was going on, and they, too, began to call on the LORD. Praise God for His mighty convicting power![20]

18. Sturgeon, *Give Me This Mountain*, 1.
19. Ma, *When the Spirit Meets the Spirits*, 78.
20. Ma, *When the Spirit Meets Spirits*, 87.

BUILDING TUDING CHURCH

As more and more people came to God, Vanderbout felt the need to have a church building where all the people could comfortably worship God. She began to pray with strong faith to build a church within Tuding. However, it was not an easy job to do because the first materials purchased cost two thousand dollars. After several months, Vanderbout wrote to her former pastor, Turnbull, regarding this project and her needs. To her surprise, Pastor Turnbull sent a check for two thousand dollars. Later, the Foreign Missions Department sent a sizable amount to build the church. Vanderbout set about purchasing property to build a new church right away.[21]

Finally, the building was sufficiently finished for dedication, even though the ceiling and the interior were not complete. The dedication service was held on December 9, 1949. Vanderbout invited Reverend Howard Osgood, the former missionary to China and the speaker at the missionary convention in Bethel Temple Church, where Vanderbout had received her call. A mass of people flooded into the service.[22]

Juan Soriano, a mountain ministry team member, was chosen to pastor this church. Why was Soriano selected as the pastor of Tuding church? Was Vanderbout not qualified to be the pastor herself? First, Soriano was enthusiastic and dedicated himself to the evangelism ministry. He was thus well suited to pastor this newly erected church. In Kankana-ey culture, men are dominant in every part of social activities. That probably influenced the selection of this leader over Vanderbout, although it was a female missionary who had endeavored to erect the church building. A native pastor was also preferred over a foreigner to lead the congregation effectively. Later, the Tuding church became a place for conducting seminars, short training of church leaders, revival meetings, and various other agendas.

SPREAD THE GOSPEL AND POWER ENCOUNTER IN TUDING

Vanderbout preached the gospel once a week in open-air services in Tuding in 1954. She proclaimed the healing power of God during the service, based on Scripture from Mark 16:15–18: "They shall lay hands on the sick, and they shall recover." She saw the need of these people and, with simple

21. Sturgeon, *Give Me This Mountain*, 111.

22. Vanderbout, "Personal Newsletter to the Foreign Mission Department."

faith in the word of God, called on her ministry team members to pray for the sick.[23]

A young boy who was fourteen years of age had ulcers on his leg. Witch doctors somewhat treated the boy, but he could not be cured. When this boy was seven years old, he had fallen, and his leg was broken right at the knee. The next five years of his life were challenging because the bones grew together and bent as the leg healed. His leg was stiff, and he could not straighten it. He could not touch the ground, which meant he could not walk. He struggled, hopping along with the help of a stick or by just crawling along on the ground, and he certainly lived a miserable life.[24] The boy's mother became a Christian because she believed in God, and the boy's parents gave up their pagan worship, determined to follow Christ. Vanderbout and her ministry team came to the boy's home to visit. Vanderbout laid her hand upon him and prayed, believing Christ could heal. This boy threw away his stick, believing in the healing power of God.[25] From then on, he no longer used his stick, and his leg straightened out little by little. The ulcers disappeared by God's power.

Many souls were saved by healing experience through God's power manifested in the ministry of Vanderbout and her team members. There was a little girl who had not been able to walk for a couple of years. She began to walk by a miracle of God. Her parents turned to Christ through their daughter's healing, and they attended the services regularly. Such testimonies of healing caused revival to grow and added to the number of believers. The crowds attending usually comprised the whole barrio population. The revival in Tuding was to shake the whole of Benguet Province, and this news was spread far and wide to sow the seed for the work to be done throughout the mountains.

SALVATION-HEALING MINISTRY IN BAGUIO CITY

Baguio City is an access point to different provinces. In fact, within a thirty-minute drive, people can even reach places where tribal people dwell near Baguio City. In 1955, Vanderbout had a plan of revival for salvation and healing in Baguio City, located six thousand feet above sea level. Vanderbout probably knew the strategy of holding a revival meeting in this city.

23. Sturgeon, *Give Me This Mountain*, 95.

24. Vanderbout, "Report on Trip to the Alsados," 3.

25. Vanderbout, "Work of Mercy in the Philippines," 3.

She went to the mayor to request a permit for the spot in the most prominent place, Burnham Park, for her revival meeting. The mayor's response was somewhat negative due to time conflicts—a carnival planned to use this place. Vanderbout again asked the mayor to consider her request. The mayor checked with his clerk to confirm the dates, and the clerk told him that the carnival was scheduled for a later date. Vanderbout thus got permission from the mayor to use that place. She almost shrieked for joy because it was the first time that this place was ever given for a religious aggregation.[26] Vanderbout finally set the March 1, 1955, date for the revival meeting. The speaker was Mrs. Ralph Byrd from America. About fifteen hundred came to the morning meetings. Through services, hundreds of newcomers accepted Christ as their personal Savior. God performed miracles of healing in different services. One girl, eighteen years of age, who suffered as a deaf-mute for twelve years, was instantly healed. During each morning and night service, the sick lined up for healing. God healed deaf-mutes by the scores; the blind could see; paralytics were healed. People suffering from tuberculosis and many other sicknesses were healed. One famous woman in the city was healed of a huge goiter. It partly diminished when she was prayed for on Saturday night, and when she came to the services Sunday morning, it had disappeared. A man twenty-eight years of age, who had been a deaf-mute all his life, was cured instantly one morning.[27] The eight days of the salvation and healing revival were marvelous in that countless people came to the Lord, and a myriad of sick people were healed. These phenomena were recognized as the work of the Holy Spirit.

SALVATION-HEALING MINISTRY IN MOUNTAIN PROVINCE

Vanderbout wanted to hold consecutive salvation and healing meetings in Mountain Province. Since the missionary had met with empirical experience of the power of healing in previous meetings, she attempted to repeat the effect in Mountain Province without fully anticipating the Holy Spirit's true empowerment.[28] During eight days of meetings in Baguio City, there was a mighty outpouring of the Holy Spirit amid services. Nearly forty were baptized in the Holy Spirit. There were several outstanding conversions of

26. Vanderbout, "Salvation-Healing Revival in Baguio City, Philippines," 2.
27. Vanderbout, "Salvation-Healing Revival in Baguio City, Philippines," 2.
28. Vanderbout, "Talubin Christians Re-Enact Conversion," 2.

distinguished government officials, including the deputy governor of the sub-province, his wife, and his daughter. The mayor of a nearby town was saved and healed from sickness. He gave a resounding testimony.

After this meeting, Vanderbout decided to evangelize further in the mountains. She loaded camping equipment, a public address system, and an electric light system into her car. The missionary and national workers drove nearly all day over rugged mountain roads into head-hunter territory. Almost the whole village came out to the meetings. God's power stirred people's hearts in the village where they held a service. The Holy Spirit moved among people, and many healing miracles were performed. Many of the new converts took a clear stand for Christ, even against persecution and the raving of the heathen priests and witch doctors. In another large village, with many surrounding villages, God gave Vanderbout and local workers a marvelous meeting of six days. Hundreds came from all different directions and filled the town marketplace to hear the gospel. For most of them, it was the first time in their lives that they had listened to the gospel. As Vanderbout recognized, this was precisely what Christ came to the world to do: to minister with power, to save the lost, and to heal the sick. Miracles continually took place. An old man from another village was carried by his friends to the meeting. He was bent over and could walk only on his hands and feet, like an animal. The man instantly stood up and walked. He gave his life to Christ and began excitedly preaching to the people. He did not return to his home but stayed at the meeting place, telling everybody what God had done for him. He almost joined the evangelistic team to share his testimony.[29]

Many sick people experienced the healing power of God. An old man who had been deaf in both ears since he was a young man was instantly healed in the service. An old woman had been blind in both eyes since 1942; she was healed and could see from both eyes. One paralyzed woman spent most of Sunday morning crawling to attend to the service. God instantly healed her, and she stood and walked across the ground to the platform to testify of God's healing power. An old, blind woman attended one meeting with her granddaughter's encouragement. God instantly opened both of her eyes, and she pointed out the lights and different objects. People in the meeting were amazed by such incidents and glorified the name of

29. Vanderbout, "Salvation-Healing Meetings in Mountain Province," in "Salvation-Healing Revival," 2–3.

Jesus Christ.[30] As a result of these meetings, believers in a village inhabited by twelve thousand people wanted to build a church. In another village, known as head-hunters, men had already started to build their church. Vanderbout planned to begin a short-term Bible school and have special classes for the new converts. God, indeed, had done a great miracle in opening up these villages.

ESTABLISHING AN ORPHANAGE

During the ministry, Vanderbout noticed that many babies were suffering from sickness. Erecting an orphanage was not entirely her intention; she did it out of necessity. As Vanderbout became known as a white missionary with a loving and caring heart for the mountain people, believers and nonbelievers sought her help for their needs, including problems with their children's sicknesses. There was a baby who was severely crippled and needed an operation almost immediately; otherwise, he would die. The mother of this baby desperately searched for a way to save her baby's life. The only person in whom the mother put her trust was the missionary. The mother pleaded with Vanderbout for help. She took the baby to her doctor in Baguio City the following day. The doctor carefully examined the baby. He said the baby's foot would be all right after five weeks of treatment. Just as the doctor said, the baby's foot recovered in exactly five weeks of treatment, and even though he had a slight limp, it was hardly noticeable. Vanderbout's sacrificial love for a little soul touched the hearts of many people, who then turned to the Lord. The news spread through the villages that such happenings frequently took place. Vanderbout tended to meet more sick children. Children who did not have places to live were also brought to Vanderbout. Many orphans were crying for help. Some children, who would undoubtedly have died, were kept alive because the missionary took them in and nursed them back to health. Vanderbout still felt the pressing need to erect a building to accommodate the children coming to her, and she began praying. Vanderbout's prayer for this need was answered through the Rotary Club of Baguio City. They donated a generous offering to build the orphanage. The new building for the orphanage was quickly finished enough to allow children to live in it in 1953. They named it Bethesda Children's Home. Undoubtedly, more children were added after the founding of

30. Vanderbout, "Salvation-Healing Meetings in Mountain Province," in "Salvation-Healing Revival," 3.

the orphanage. While operating the orphanage, Vanderbout had an exotic experience. An unwanted child was put in a cage in the village of Bua; the child was put there by the father and stepmother. The child was in a cage for many days—no one could tell how long. The child's body was deformed, and her hair covered her face like a jungle creature. The child also had an oversized chest, clubfoot, a paralyzed right hand, and very big eyes. The child was brought to Vanderbout. The missionary's compassion and love saved the life of this little child.[31]

Another of Vanderbout's testimonies was about twin boys whom their parents abandoned. People in the mountain believed twins were bad luck, so these boys were left on the hut floor with a thin blanket. Two of Vanderbout's workers found the twin boys and carried them out. When they got to Tuding, the children were already blue and near death. However, the boys' lives were saved. Vanderbout then had twenty-two children in her orphanage.[32]

A significant story was about how a twelve-year-old boy from the jail in Baguio became a family member of the Bethesda Children's Home. After a short while, because of outside influences, he went astray. He was repeatedly in and out of the city jail several times. At one time, he spent five years at Muntinlupa National Prison, a maximum-security facility in Manila. While this boy was there, he met the Lord through a meaningful message from someone there and was transformed. When he returned to Bethesda Children's Home, he was a new person, and he even sought to go to Luzon Bible Institute out of his desire to serve the Lord. This boy grew to become an excellent minister for God's kingdom.[33] The first child who entered the Bethesda Children's Home, Gervacio Tavera, Jr., later became an ordained minister and one of the most able interpreters in the Philippines. Many of the children in the orphanage became marvelous Christians and Christian workers.[34] For Vanderbout, erecting Bethesda Children's Home was not just establishing an institution for social work as others did, nor was it merely a place for homeless, sick, and poor children to live together. Vanderbout's intention for the Children's Home was to make children grow in the living word of God so that they would become messengers of Christ.

31. Ma, *When the Spirit Meets the Spirits*, 83.
32. Vanderbout, "Work of Mercy in the Philippines," 3.
33. Vanderbout, "Personal Newsletter to the Foreign Mission Department."
34. Vanderbout, "Report on Trip to the Alsados," 1.

DEVELOPMENT OF CHILDREN'S MINISTRY

Vanderbout continued to develop a ministry for children and envisioned children as future workers for the mountain ministry. Vanderbout had the particular intention of organizing activities with this aim in mind. Thus, in 1961, the first kid's camp held in the Philippines emerged. At this time, the concept of kid's camp was unfamiliar to local churches in the Philippines. About seventy children came to this initial kid's camp, and thirty-five received Christ as their personal Savior. About ten were baptized in the Holy Spirit. Unusual experiences that children had included having visions of the Lord, feeling God's sweet presence during prayer, and so on. God mightily poured out his Spirit upon these precious boys and girls. Kid's camp was then to serve as an avenue for others to meet the Lord.[35]

Vanderbout organized the first Missionette Club in the Philippines at the Tuding church. Its purpose was to train children and teenagers to be missionaries in the future. Vanderbout initiated these programs for all children, and children were intensively trained to memorize Bible verses to prepare themselves to be soldiers of Christ. In the opening ceremony, an impressive candlelight and pledge signing service was conducted for twenty-two Missionettes and thirteen Junior Missionettes. District officers and some sectional presbyters attended the service. Each girl proudly wore her Missionette uniform, consisting of a navy blue skirt, white blouse, and light blue vest. The Missionette emblem was embroidered on the left side of the vest. Occasionally Vanderbout had special prayer meetings in which children and teenagers were spiritually saturated or bathed in prayer. The Holy Spirit baptized some children. Later, many children became beautiful Christian ministers.

TRAINING YOUNG PEOPLE

In 1962, Vanderbout began to train young people with burdens for serving the Lord. They were recruited and sent to a Bible school. As Vanderbout continued with the mountain ministry, she came to feel the need for more hands to reach out to more unreached nonbelievers. She also felt the need to train native young people to reach their people. Four of them from mountain provinces graduated from a Bible school and were involved in pioneering works. Others graduated and became evangelists in areas deep

35. Vanderbout, "Personal Newsletter to the Foreign Mission Department."

in the mountains where no Assemblies of God workers had ever penetrated. These young people were enthusiastic to hike through dense forests to preach the gospel despite difficulties and danger.[36] When Vanderbout started the mountain work, there were only two national ministers for the mountain ministry. But ten years later, twenty-two full-time national workers were involved in the mountain ministry, and fifteen young people were ready to go to a Bible school to prepare for future work. The mountain ministry continued with vitality and abundant fruits through the young ministers.

ANALYSIS

In this section, I have presented narrative accounts of the ministry of Vanderbout in the mountain regions of the northern Philippines. It will be appropriate to analyze a few essential elements that made her ministry successful and made it possible to spread the gospel among the Kankana-ey tribe.

Power Message

As a Pentecostal, she approached the animistic people with a powerful message and demonstration of God's power. As delineated above, God's power is revealed in various incidents, such as healing and casting out demons. It was indeed efficacious to bring these people to Christ because there was a common worldview found between the two groups, the Pentecostals and the animistic people. In explaining this, tribal people believed that their gods and deceased spirits obtained power to heal the sick and bless their lives. Thus, when there is a sick person, they implore the spirit to cure her or through the help of a mediator (priest). The people perceive that ordinary people cannot communicate with the gods or spirits, but only priests can. Therefore, when the power of God was demonstrated among them, they realized and recognized the power of a Christian God, whose power is greater than that of their gods. It was indeed a turning point for them toward Christ. Often, they offer many sacrifices until the sick get healed. Due to offering sacrifices repeatedly, they have to borrow money from their relatives or friends to buy sacrificial animals. Experiencing God's healing

36. Vanderbout, "Personal Newsletter to the Foreign Mission Department."

touch without offering any sacrifice was new to them. In my observation, the power encounter was the key factor in winning the souls for Christ.

Recognition of Women Leadership

In tribal culture, it is challenging to accommodate women as leaders of a village or community. Men's authority has been prevalent in that culture and traditionally inherent. When there are special occasions, such as conducting funerals, wedding ceremonies, or ritual practices, male leaders are assumed to lead. Throughout my experience in close association with them, the male is dominantly in the leadership position. In such a cultural setting, it is incredible that the woman missionary was to be a leading figure. A single female missionary had settled in a notorious place (Tuding) where local ministers felt reluctant to live and associate with the people there. Her determination to live in such a place perhaps showed native leaders her potential capability to work with their people. Probably, this exemplary attitude caused native pastors to assist and join her ministry. Secondly, using spiritual gifts was an attractive force to follow her. As described in the preceding pages, what happened in Vanderbout's ministry reflected the true Pentecostal atmosphere depicted in the book of Acts. When the apostles were empowered, they performed diverse miracles. Those people, having seen such an extraordinary occurrence, followed the apostles and became instruments of God's mission. The apostles naturally were to become the leading figures. In this sense, spiritual gifts do not directly serve to bring them into the leadership position but could be a supporting factor. Thirdly, I assume that Vanderbout's zeal and great ambition to spread the gospel among the mountain villages moved the hearts of the local pastors to support and follow her. She was bold enough to invade those pagan regions where the people had never known Christ and heard his name. Breaking into an air-tight tradition with a foreign gospel was tremendously difficult. This was an adamant will to fulfill the divine task done by a so-called self-leader.

Assistance of Local Ministry Team

Looking at her ministry, Vanderbout had an incredible ministry team. There were sincere and committed pastors to assist her work. Indeed, she could not speak the native dialect perfectly, meaning she needed someone to interpret her sermons and have deep conversations with church members. Also, she was unfamiliar with geography and trails in the mountains. This indicates that there must have been someone who could accompany her always, wherever she went. It was a simple assistance from her ministry team but an important one.

A few local pastors who were oriented by her spiritual leadership experienced the empowerment of the Holy Spirit and could exercise spiritual gifts in the worship service. It would be a great help to her ministry to be effective, as Vanderbout, without assistance from her ministry team, would not be that great, no matter how empowered she was.

Leadership Training

Vanderbout, amid busy activities, did not neglect to train local leaders. She sent prominent and ambitious young leaders to a Bible school for future ministry in the mountains. As indicated earlier, she saw the need for local ministers to join this ministry as it was impossible for her alone to hike every corner of various mountain regions. Besides that, she was a foreigner who could depart anytime due to a particular circumstance. Another reason would be that it would be much more effective for local pastors to minister to their people in their vernacular language. It was a marvelous investment for the tribal ministry of successful church planting and evangelism.

CONCLUDING REMARKS

Many villages were entirely transformed because Vanderbout was willing to lay down her life. Foxes had holes, and birds had nests, but she, like the Son of Man, had no place to settle. She fearlessly entered pagan villages that practiced "head-hunting."[37] She spread the vital and precious message of Christ. Vanderbout trusted that God would protect her from harm. Her ministry among the Kankana-ey tribe and other tribes seems inexhaustible and is not recounted in this chapter. The desire of her heart to live and minister in the mountains was fulfilled, and with it came satisfaction in knowing that her work was not in vain. Indeed, she would receive her

37. Head-hunting was prevalent among the mountain tribal people during those days. Particularly the Bontok tribe practices it exceedingly. It has two purposes: one is to take revenge, and another is to show men's bravery to the one they love.

crown in heaven, and her work would not go unnoticed by the Lord. This was her reflection in 1962.

From the initial time of Vanderbout's ministry, 1947, until 1959, eight churches were constructed under her direction. There were over one hundred preaching points throughout various mountain areas. She reached more than one hundred villages with the gospel. In 1955, Vanderbout started to work in villages of the head-hunting mountain people, a singular accomplishment of the thirteen years of her service in the mountains. Besides the ministry of evangelism and church planting, Vanderbout did not neglect training devoted young people. As a result of her labor, approximately one hundred young people from the mountains went to Bible school, and most became ministers to reach their people. Vanderbout, out of necessity, erected an orphanage to care for poor, neglected, and abandoned children. She took care of fifteen of the original children of the orphanage.[38]

After thirteen years of mountain ministry as an Assemblies of God missionary, she departed the denomination, following in a new direction. She married the local pastor, Juan Soriano, who had accompanied her to assist her ministry. According to the Assemblies of God Foreign Missions Department in Springfield, Missouri, that arrangement was not permissible. The policy held for all female missionaries. So, in 1966, Vanderbout resigned from her missionary position under the auspices of the Foreign Missions Department and the Philippines General Council of the Assemblies of God.[39] It is impossible to present a complete picture of Vanderbout's life among those she loved, but the Lord directed her life from the day of her arrival in the Philippines.

38. Vanderbout, "Personal Newsletter to the Foreign Mission Department."

39. Vanderbout, "Personal Newsletter to the Foreign Mission Department."

4

Women at Yoido Full Gospel Church

Pentecostalism in a Confucian Society

INTRODUCTION

It is agreed that the gender bias against females is partly attributed to the fall of the five-hundred-year rule of the Chosun Dynasty in 1910. The dynasty took Confucianism as the national ideology to such an extreme extent that some later developments distorted the original intent.[1] One aspect of the Confucian ideology was the unequal status of men and women, which led to the notion that males can achieve more and are better than females. Until recently, its impact lingered in Korean society in the preference of boys over girls, eventually creating a gender imbalance in the national population.

In this gender-biased Korean culture, the arrival of Christianity challenged this long-standing cultural value by promoting education and social roles among girls and women. The rise of Pentecostalism significantly strengthened this cultural challenge, best exemplified by the impact of Yoido Full Gospel Church, founded by David Yonggi Cho. The most decisive program was Cho's radical decision to appoint women as leaders of his popular cell group system. This was an alternative to his original intention to nominate men to cell leadership, which met with unexpected resistance from male lay leaders. The current senior pastor, Younghoon

1. Ackerson, "Korean Confucianism," 100–110.

Lee, continues strengthening the predominantly female leadership of the cell group system.

This section first explores the pervasive influence of Confucianism on Korean society, particularly on the attitude of gender preference. It then addresses how Cho decided to select the women to be leaders of the cell groups in the Korean social and cultural context. Then, it probes the implications of this decision to the church's growth in various stages and discusses the structure of three cell leaderships, the cell group system and the main components of a typical home cell meeting, and its contribution to church growth.

INFLUENCE OF CONFUCIANISM ON RELIGION AND CULTURE IN KOREA

The five-century dominance of Confucianism over the Chosun Dynasty has profoundly impacted the formation of social and cultural values. Strictly speaking, Confucianism offers moral teachings that are valuable to systematically sustaining a society. On the other hand, it does not provide spiritual direction as much as Buddhism does.

Moral Values of Confucianism

An essential, valuable supposition of Confucianism is to be faithful and respectful in a relationship with various groups of people to minimize conflicts and to aspire to maintain a balanced collaboration. Specifically, "the virtues of five different relationships to maintain harmony in life: the right relationship between father and son, ruler and subject, husband and wife, elder and younger, and between friends."[2] It also teaches the virtue of courtesy so that, for instance, students would speak politely to their teachers. In the same way, females must talk more tenderly than males in public places and walk behind men.[3] The Confucian ideal assumes that "society can effectively work toward the collective good" under two conditions:[4] (1) everyone fulfills his or her allocated duties within the societal hierarchy, and

2. Kim, *Women of Korea*, 53.

3. Baker, *Dimensions of Asian Spirituality*, 46. See also Yao, *Introduction to Confucianism*, 115.

4. Baker, *Dimensions of Asian Spirituality*, 42.

(2) the mutual responsibility of the benefactor toward the beneficiary and the beneficiary's responsibility toward the benefactor is dutifully fulfilled.

For instance, the appropriate rapport between father and son is ruled by love. For the father, love is displayed by parental care. The Confucian assumption is that a wonderful father provides his son with adequate food, accommodations, outfits, schooling, and suitable ethical direction, whether the son is a little boy or an adult. Likewise, a son must exhibit love by practicing obedience, respect, and "filial piety" to his father.[5]

Impact of Teaching of Filial Piety in Korea

Confucianism has generally influenced the shaping of the minds and lives of Koreans, especially in the area of "filial piety." As briefly mentioned above, the correct relationship between the father and the son is built upon the son's submission and respect for the father. The son's school achievement is considered an honor for the entire family. A son is a symbol of the family heredity, tasked to fulfill the "ancestral rituals" and to support the "parents in their old age." Looking after his aged parents is the mark of a good son. The son embodies "family pride." For this reason, parental duty includes providing the best education to the son, even if it costs a substantial financial sacrifice.[6] This relationship continues after the father's death. The son must demonstrate the obligation of his care and respect to his deceased father through the appropriate and dutiful performance of ceremonies of filial piety. This also serves as the son's expression of his gratitude for his father's role in bringing the son into the world and his efforts to nurture and raise him. This generational solidarity extends to further generations as the rituals demonstrate the son's gratefulness for giving life to his father, to ancestors, e.g., his father's father, his father's grandfather, and so on.[7] And this duty is the responsibility and privilege of the male descendants. It is said during Korea's long Chosun Dynasty, only males in a direct line of descent could lead memorial services for departed ancestors. That tradition survived in the twenty-first century.

In most Korean families today, although a daughter keeps her father's family name as her surname even after she marries, she usually cannot lead the memorial services for her deceased parents or grandparents. Moreover,

5. Baker, *Dimensions of Asian Spirituality*, 42–43.

6. Clark, *Culture and Customs of Korea*, 158.

7. Baker, *Dimensions of Asian Spirituality*, 43.

her children will usually take her husband's family name. Therefore, the family name will disappear within two generations without a son carrying it on. Even worse, there will be no one who can organize and lead the memorial services necessary to keep the memory of ancestors alive and to provide visual reminders that their descendants continue to appreciate all the ancestors did for them.[8]

The eldest son's responsibility is greater than that of the younger ones. He is expected to live with his father and mother even after marriage. My husband is the eldest of five siblings. My parents-in-law longed for a time for us to live with them, even though it was impossible during our missionary years. As they got older, they hoped we would conclude our missionary service and live with them. But that dream was never fulfilled before they passed away.

Of course, in a society where a social security system is not entirely in place, the survival of the elderly depends totally on the son's care and support. Although there are some cases where the eldest sons have left their parents behind and migrated elsewhere, they regularly send financial support to look after their parents. In such cases, the younger siblings would relocate their parents to their urban flats, even if they are small enough for the increasing number of families. A massive exodus of people from large cities to rural hometowns and villages during special days, such as the Moon Festival (*chusok*), partly concerns family expectations and obligations. Traditionally, the ritual to honor their deceased ancestors is at the center of family reunions. The family reunion at their parent's sixtieth and seventieth birthdays also expresses this family tradition and obligation.[9]

Favoritism of Sons

In Korea, some women with only daughters invariably hope to have another child with a hope for a son. And if the next child turns out to be a girl again, they will try repeatedly until they finally have a son. I am the eldest of five in my family. My father was very disappointed when my mother gave birth to the first child, a female (that is me). He did not even give me a name for fifteen days. My father's desire to have a son never diminished. Thus, my mother kept on giving birth to three more girls before having a son, who was the last.

8. Baker, *Dimensions of Asian Spirituality*, 44.
9. Baker, *Dimensions of Asian Spirituality*, 43.

Old folks maintain an expectation that a grown-up daughter will marry and transfer to her husband's home to be a new family member. Thus, girls are expected to learn cooking, sewing, and caring for children as future mothers. Due to such reasons, a majority of girls stay at home to help their mother with childcare for younger siblings and house chores, including the "laundry by pounding clothes on flat rocks beside the village stream." They begin doing this housework when they turn only five or six, although this no longer applies today, especially in cities.[10] Nonetheless, even today, the parents regard it as most successful for their daughters to marry a man from a decent and reputable family.

The government population policy further aggravated this tendency. At the start of Korea's thrust for "economic modernization, the government launched a nationwide campaign to arrest the postwar population explosion through better family planning."[11] Although resources were harshly restricted many years ago, the Ministry of Health and Social Affairs would hire staff for family planning in the furthest regions of the country. In the Poksu District of Kumsan County, the district headquarters appointed an employee called Mrs. Kim to encourage the residents of South Valley Hamlet to limit the number of children they wanted to have. She educated people to use various contraceptive devices and methods.[12] The immediate challenge was the long-held preference for sons over daughters. The sons are responsible for looking after their parents, especially when they get old. They must also continue the family heritage in every aspect, including the faithful performance of family rituals to look after the deceased ancestors. Mrs. Kim's hard work was well recognized in educating the women of Poksu about birth control and, more importantly, the value of life.[13] However, she faced her challenges. Her mother-in-law anticipated Mrs. Kim would have a son, as they only had two daughters: Mr. Kim was her eldest child, and the mother-in-law was upset that he had no son to carry on the family line. She would mention that the Kim family had enjoyed a succession of strong, bright sons for many generations and that only now, since this daughter-in-law, who had newfangled ideas about family planning, had been introduced, was this honorable family tradition being broken. She

10. Clark, *Culture and Customs of Korea*, 158.

11. Clark, *Culture and Customs of Korea*, 158.

12. It appears as Mrs. Kim in the book, not in full name; Clark, *Culture and Customs of Korea*, 157.

13. Clark, *Culture and Customs of Korea*, 157.

disapproved of family planning and would often tell her daughter-in-law that it was wrong to limit families to two children, indicating the best insurance was to have sons, as always, and the Kim family was most unfortunate to have this stubborn daughter-in-law who thought government policies were more important than the family's needs.[14]

Her mother-in-law pressured her and made Mrs. Kim feel she had "failed" her most outstanding fundamental family obligation. Soon after having that thought, she was pregnant with her third child and "in due course bore a stalwart son." Finally, the Kims discontinued their efforts to have more children. However, Mrs. Kim later confessed that if the baby had been a girl, she would have attempted a fourth. "Being a good daughter-in-law was the most important thing of all, even for an award-winning family planning worker."[15]

Gender Inequality

The practice of male preference extends to the entire life spectrum. In Koreans' minds and life patterns, the superior value is placed on men over women, especially in public settings. The Confucian convention stipulates one of the five critical human relations as "the one between a husband and a wife, and that conjugal relationship is supposed to be governed by respect for gender differences in roles and responsibilities." It denotes that husbands should lead their wives, and wives must obey their husbands. This presumes an image of women to be frail. They are to be the recipient of provision and protection from their husbands. They are confined to domestic life.[16] South Korea has one of the lowest voting-women ratios among industrialized states. Male CEOs control the business realm. There are only a few women CEOs and even fewer women ministers in churches in Korea.[17]

Today's egalitarianism seriously challenges the Confucian ideology of maintaining a social status quo. Confucians promote harmony as more important than equality. The Confucian understanding of "harmony" is attained through various members of society to faithfully fulfill their expected duties and submit to the superiors within the hierarchy. Everyone

14. Clark, *Culture and Customs of Korea*, 159.
15. Clark, *Culture and Customs of Korea*, 159.
16. Son, "Confucianism and the Lack of the Development," 325–35.
17. Baker, *Dimensions of Asian Spirituality*, 44–45.

has different work and tasks, accompanying "differences in status within their families and communities."[18] It further emphasizes that Confucians insisted that with human nature being what it is, such acquiescence would usually be instinctive, a spontaneous result of respect and appreciation for those who lead others, whether parents or community leaders. Confucian moral obligations were not seen as inhibiting normal human behavior but rather were understood as natural expressions of gratitude to those who have helped make us what we are.[19]

Korea in the present day provides many more chances for females than in the previous generations. Public education is provided up to high school for both sexes nationwide. Many girls continue their education at universities and graduate schools, and families sacrificially support their education. "Korean women are shedding many aspects of second-class citizenship," but they continue under restrictions and expectations. Their lives primarily focus on a good marriage, and everything else is secondary to this. Although many young females are defiant of such an expectation, they are the exception rather than the rule. Though they are university professors and selected government officers, it is discovered that ordinary family life is crucial to obtaining esteem from the community. Females in high-status positions still must subject themselves to this social norm. They are identified as someone's daughter, wife, and mother.[20]

In summary, the ethics of Confucian has profoundly shaped Korean culture, people's everyday lives, and norms. The moral foundation of the limitations on females is focused on Confucian philosophy. Restrictions on liberty for females are explained in many Confucian manuscripts and "treatises" by significant philosophers in the "early Chosun dynasty." For women to be respectful, they must be humble, quietly isolated, faithful, dedicated to "motherhood," and even faithful to their husbands after they die.[21]

DAVID YONGGI CHO AND YOIDO FULL GOSPEL CHURCH

David Yonggi Cho, the founding and now senior pastor emeritus of Yoido Full Gospel Church, was born in 1936 and raised in a Buddhist home.

18. Baker, *Dimensions of Asian Spirituality*, 45.
19. Baker, *Dimensions of Asian Spirituality*, 45.
20. Clark, *Culture and Customs of Korea*, 160.
21. Deuchler, *Confucian Transformation of Korea*, 231–81.

When he was a teenager, he suffered from terminal tuberculosis. With limited access to medical services, he was left to die. One day, a girl visited him and introduced Jesus. Cho, who was physically feeble, opened his heart and accepted Christ as his personal Savior. He also experienced an astonishing healing from God.

In 1956, he entered Full Gospel Bible College (for a two-year diploma program) to receive theological training. Unfortunately, in the winter of 1957, Cho had severe flu. Mrs. Jashil Choi, Cho's classmate, nursed him with prayer for about two weeks. He soon recovered. This brought them closer to each other as ministry partners. Later, Choi became Cho's mother-in-law.

Three Stages of the Growth of the Church

The initial stage of Cho's pastoral ministry began in May 1958, soon after he graduated from Bible College. He and Choi pioneered a tent church on the outskirts of Seoul called Bulkwang-dong. Cho was the leading pastor, while Choi served as his associate. Cho regularly preached on Sundays. At his first preaching, there were only five people: Choi and her three children and a farmer's aging widow. During this pioneering period, Cho became interested in healing ministry. He read many books on healing by Pentecostal writers, including Oral Roberts. Most books included Bible expositions, which helped Cho to understand the basis for healing. This was a significant breakthrough as some "guest lecturers at the Bible College said that the age of miracles had passed with the last of the twelve apostles."[22]

Cho held summer crusades in the first year (1958). Remarkably, radical conversions and healings occurred. An old man had lost his hearing during the Japanese colonization in Korea when he refused to obey the orders of the Japanese. Out of anger, "the Japanese had thrust a chopstick into each of the man's ears, bursting his eardrums." That cost his hearing, and he had not heard for fifteen years. During the crusade, suddenly, he began to hear again. The next day, he brought his entire family, including his grandchildren, to the campaign. Numerous people converted to Christ during the crusade. The tent church kept on growing in number. Cho strongly desired to move his church to a larger and better facility as the tent church was bursting at the seams. He began constructing a new church building in the downtown Seodaemoon area and completed it in February 1962.[23]

22. Hurston, *Growing the World's Largest Church*, 22.

23. A couple of American Assembles of God missionaries provided financial support. And the new location, Seodaemoon, is a city area which provides access to the city center.

The second stage began after moving his church to the new downtown location. American evangelist Sam Todd held a revival meeting in September 1962 while the construction continued. A large crowd attended the revival meetings, and many had experiences of God's marvelous presence and miracles. The church's fifteen hundred seats were fully occupied.[24] In the same year, Cho was ordained by the Korean Assemblies of God, the largest Pentecostal denomination in Korea. The church's membership reached three thousand in 1964.

The third stage started when Cho moved his church to Yoido Island in 1973. The tent church began in 1958 in Daejodong with five members and snowballed to six hundred members by 1961. In the Seodaemoon facility, the church continued to grow in number and needed a larger space to accommodate the growing congregation. Then Cho decided to build another larger facility on Yoido Island, a newly developing financial district away from the center of Seoul. Despite economic struggles and some members' opposition, the church started construction and completed it in September 1973. The church grew even more rapidly after moving to the new location. In 1979, the membership reached one hundred thousand; in November 1980, it reached two hundred thousand; in 1985, it reached five hundred thousand, and in 1992, it grew to seven hundred thousand.[25]

Characteristics of Growth

Significant church growth took place in Korea in the 1970s and 1980s, and at the center of this explosive growth was the example and influence of Yoido Full Gospel Church.[26] This section briefly highlights the characteristics of church growth, which Cho personally enumerated. Firstly, Cho, the church leader, strongly desired his church to grow. Growing up in a Buddhist family, a local church symbolized the living God in each community. As a local expression of the organic and living Body of Christ, he firmly believed that the church "must" grow. He concluded that the attitude of the pastor is critical to church growth. Secondly, the message from the church should be positive and uplifting, that Jesus is the ultimate provider of all our needs. In Cho's mind, the church must preach the message of hope. After the war between North and South Korea in 1950–53, the country was

24. Hurston, *Growing the World's Largest Church*, 25–27.

25. Church Growth International, *Church Growth Manual*, 45.

26. Ma, "Korean," 279.

devastated by a lack of food, clothing, and shelter. More importantly, the people had lost hope for a living. They needed to hear a message of hope for tomorrow. Thirdly, Cho believed the church's growth would never occur without prayer. Testimonies of God's answer to prayers were widely shared in home groups, sermons, and publications. The church started the Friday all-night prayer meetings and prayer mountains emphasizing fasting. Fourthly, it was the tangible experience of the presence of the Holy Spirit. The church inspired the members to expect and gain an experience of the fullness of the Holy Spirit (or "Full Gospel"). Encounters with God enabled the members to grow in faith and in love, which was quickly translated into their evangelistic zeal. This considerably contributed to the growth of the church. Fifthly, the church developed an extensive mission engagement in local areas and overseas by providing evangelism, church planting, and relief for humanitarian and community services. The dynamic cell group system also contributed to the church's growth. People who attended the church wanted a more intimate fellowship to develop a sense of community. Sunday services offered formal worship but rarely provided meaningful opportunities for close fellowship.[27] The last point will be elaborated below.

CELL GROUP SYSTEM OF YOIDO FULL GOSPEL CHURCH

The organization of the cell group system primarily led by the laity did not come together quickly, as the "teaching" role in the Confucian world only came from the social elite. The women's leadership of the cell system understandably came after much struggle on the part of each party involved: Cho himself, the church, and the society.

Cho's "Conversion"

As the senior pastor, Cho believed he had to take on all the ministerial responsibilities himself. When the second era of his church, the Seodaemoon era, began, he preached at two services each Sunday. However, the frequency quickly increased as the church constantly grew. In addition, he also preached at the daily dawn prayer meetings and the Wednesday evening services. He also conducted wedding and funeral services, was

27. Ook, "Message of Hope," 4–5.

involved in pastoral counseling, and baptized people almost every week (once he baptized three hundred people in the water). He even picked up guest speakers from the airport and interpreted their sermons. Once, while he was interpreting for a guest preacher, his legs shivered, and he fell to the floor. Deacons immediately took him to the hospital. A doctor examined him and said, "This man is completely drained!" Cho realized that he could not undertake all the church work by himself.[28]

Cho spent his recovery time reading the Bible and contemplating a solution for the critical shortage of church workers. He read Exod 18:13–26 and found out that Moses faced a similar challenge. He listened to all the matters people brought to him for judgment, which continued daily. He also read Acts 2:42–46 and noted that the believers had gathered in different houses to break bread and share apostolic teaching. Thousands of early Christians had home meetings. Priscilla and Aquila had church meetings in their home, as did Nympha and Philemon, along with his family (Rom 16:3–5; 1 Cor 16:19; Col 4:15; Phlm 1–2). "Cho was convinced that an effective way of church work was to share responsibilities with deacons and lay leaders. Cho soon called for a meeting among lay leaders (primarily male) and shared his findings through the scriptural readings and his plan to appoint lay leaders to organize and lead home meetings."[29] However, they were not open to Cho's plan:

> One deacon stated that he was too tired to lead a meeting at the end of the day. Another insisted that some groups would get proud, break away, and start their own churches. A third lay leader remarked that it sounded biblical, but they had not been trained for anything like this. This plan was not part of traditional church activity. "Besides," he informed Dr. Cho, "that's what we pay you for." The meeting ended with the leaders' suggestion: "Why don't you get away and take a long vacation?"[30]

Cho came back home from that meeting with discouragement. His effort to have revolutionary home groups led by mostly male lay leaders failed. While he was going through a despondency, Choi, his mother-in-law, and a group of women came to him and suggested he have female lay leaders to lead home cell groups. Cho was unwilling to consider the suggestion due to the traditional Korean bias against women. They were viewed

28. Hurston, *Growing the World's Largest Church*, 82–83.

29. Hurston, *Growing the World's Largest Church*, 83–84.

30. Hurston, *Growing the World's Largest Church*, 84.

as inferior to men, and their leadership potential was not valued. He was also mindful of particular scripture passages.[31] Not convinced initially, Cho spent time praying before making up his mind. When Cho prayed, he was prompted by the Spirit about how many women were part of Jesus' ministry. He accounts for his "conversion" with God over the issue like this:[32]

> "Yonggi, from whom were you born?" the LORD asked Cho.
> "From woman, LORD," I responded.
> "And on whose lap were you nurtured?"
> "Woman, LORD."
> "And who followed me throughout my ministry and helped to meet my needs?"
> "Women," I said.
> "Who stayed until the last minutes of my crucifixion?"
> "Women."
> "And who came to anoint my body in the tomb?"
> "The women."
> "Who were the first witnesses to my resurrection?"
> "Mary Magdalene and others, women."
> "To all my questions, you have answered, 'Woman.' Then why are you afraid of women? During my earthly ministry, I was surrounded by dear, wonderful women. So why shouldn't my body, the Church, also be surrounded and supported by women?"

Cho conceded, "What else could I do? The Lord had clarified that His will was to use women in the Church."[33] After this conviction, Cho approached the Women's Fellowship and officially informed them of his intention to appoint women leaders. They were to lead home cell group meetings. According to Cho, their response was positive. They said, "Tell us what to do, and we will obey and do the work."[34] So, the famous cell-group system was born with women leaders leading it.

Structure of Cell Group System

A cell group is the smallest pastoral unit and the fundamental component of the church. A cell is typically composed of ten to twelve families. By

31. Hurston, *Growing the World's Largest Church*, 85.

32. Hurston, *Growing the World's Largest Church*, 84–85. See also Lee, *Holy Spirit Movement in Korea*, 96.

33. Hyatt, "Spirit-Filled Women," 233–62.

34. Hurston, *Growing the World's Largest Church*, 85.

2009, 14,888 cell units met weekly in homes in various city sections.[35] The metropolitan area is divided into 20 large districts, 313 sub-districts, and 4,374 branches.[36]

Each home cell unit is ideally composed of 8 to 15 households. A new cell unit begins forming if the number exceeds the limit.[37] Cell groups are allocated to geographic regions. For areas far from the main church, regional chapels are opened for various worship services, including early morning prayers. This also helps to monitor and guide the cell system effectively.[38] Of the above-indicated cell groups, 96 percent are led by female members. The church has 634 full-time pastors and 400 elders who manage various ministries, particularly the cell group ministry.[39] Although it is still called "cell" or "home group," it is neither a social gathering nor a home fellowship meeting. A section comprises twenty-five to ninety home cell units, which a pastoral member leads.

A home cell unit leader conducts weekly meetings, frequently aided by an assistant leader. The weekly meeting moves among the members' homes. A couple of reasons for this arrangement are found in the New Testament. Firstly, believers in the book of Acts had gatherings "from house to house" (Acts 2:46), denoting that various families hosted early church meetings. Secondly, women played a unique role in the life and ministry of Jesus. Cho was convinced, "We believe that when Christians worship God in a home, that home is blessed." While the members had complete confidence in Cho's leadership and vision, he frequently and publicly attributed particular importance to the cell leaders. In response, cell members committed themselves to pray specifically for their host or hostess of the cell meetings. When a member still young in the faith falls ill or encounters hardship, the family is usually hesitant to host a cell group meeting in their homes. The cell leader and mature members encourage the family to open their homes so that the members can pray for the family's needs, be it for healing or

35. Douglas, *Yonggi Cho and the Korean Pentecostal Movement*, 16–34. See also Hurston, *Growing the World's Largest Church*, 85.

36. Lee, *Holy Spirit Movement in Korea*, 106. See also his article, "Life and Ministry of David Yonggi Cho and Yoido Full Gospel Church," 16.

37. Hurston and Hurston, *Caught in the Web*, 29–30.

38. Comskey, "Rev. Cho's Cell Groups and Dynamics of Church Growth," 143–57.

39. Lee, "Life and Ministry of David Yonggi Cho and Yoido Full Gospel Church," 16. See also Lee, *Holy Spirit Movement in Korea*, 106–7.

finances. Commonly, no home is supposed to host a cell group meeting more than once monthly.[40]

Qualifications for the Cell Group Leader

Cell leaders are the key to the success of the given cell group ministry. For this reason, the church has established criteria for selecting cell leaders. Firstly, cell leaders must have adequate knowledge of the word of God. He or she needs to be well prepared to teach the cell members. Secondly, they need to share the church's passion for church growth and desire to be used by the Holy Spirit. Thirdly, the cell leaders must be Spirit-filled so that they can, in turn, assist their cell members to be filled with the Holy Spirit. Fourthly, they must have a vision for the cell group. They are encouraged to pray to develop a vision for new souls to be led to Christ, which would result in the growth of the cell group. Fifthly, they ought to continually strengthen their Christian faith: not to be easily despondent but to enable the cell members to grow in trust for their lives to be transformed. Sixthly, the cell group leaders must be role models to the members by living exemplary lives.[41]

Equipping the Cell Group Leaders

The church provides primary training to new cell leaders and continuing training to existing leaders. The church's education division organizes the direct leadership program, the eight-week "cell leaders' college." Staff members of the college and regional pastors provide training based on the established curriculum on Sunday afternoons. The continuing activity occurs during the "semiannual conference of sectional and cell leaders" held in the spring and fall of each year. Initially, the conference lasted three days, with inspirational messages, guidelines for cell group management, and fresh new worship songs. However, in recent years, due to the large number of cell leaders, the church has reduced the conferences to a single meeting consisting of an educational lecture and a stimulating message from Cho.

40. Hurston, *Growing the World's Largest Church*, 89–90.

41. Myung and Hong, "Church Growth and All Groups," 95–96.

The same program is repeated to accommodate many cell leaders. During both times, the main sanctuary is packed to the maximum capacity.[42]

The Role the Cell Group Leaders Play

The roles of the cell leaders are the following: (1) to be accountable for the members of their cell unit; (2) join every Wednesday training session through videotape, from 5:00 to 6:00 in the afternoon; (3) conduct every week home cell meetings where the leader provides a Bible study based on the Wednesday session and also leading a prayer time; (4) being active, together with cell group members, in inviting nonbelievers to cell group meetings and church worship services; (5) to "check at least once a week with their section leaders to keep its status chart current at the church office, and submit a weekly report of their previous meetings. The report includes dates for the incoming meetings, visitation finished, significant prayer requests of any member, the amount of collection received, and the number of new believers; and finally, (6) attending the semi-annual training conference for cell leaders."[43]

Role of the Sectional and District Leaders

Sectional leaders are appointed among cell leaders who have served effectively for two years. They typically manage between three and eight cell groups. The expectations of the section leaders include: (1) connecting between pastors and the cell leaders; (2) winning souls as much as they can; (3) having the "financial resources" to support the church; (4) having their own home adequate to host "a monthly meeting with all the leaders of the section"; and (5) expecting to be spiritually and emotionally mature.[44] Additional responsibilities are the following:

> One responsibility of section leaders is the ongoing training of cell group leaders. They do this most often by modeling, especially with cell leaders in ministry visits. Also, there is a monthly leaders' meeting in each section, when the group leaders of that area meet with their staff pastor in the home of the section leader for

42. Hurston, *Growing the World's Largest Church*, 75.
43. Hurston and Hurston, *Caught in the Web*, 39–40.
44. Hurston, *Growing the World's Largest Church*, 76.

> prayer and ministry. After this meeting, the staff pastor usually goes with the section leader and group leaders to visit the homes and businesses of those in that area undergoing the most difficulty. As the staff pastor ministers and prays with these people, section and group leaders often write notes and learn by observing.[45]

Many section leaders regularly speak with their home cell leaders on the phone. The frequency ranges from daily to weekly. The section leaders then set aside one day a week to visit the cell leaders and members who face serious struggles or difficulties.[46]

District leaders are prayerfully selected among assistant pastors by the senior pastor at an annual meeting. Some are ordained, others are licensed ministers, but all have adequate ministry experience. They also need to demonstrate sound spiritual maturity and competency in pastoral work. Among others, they are mainly responsible in three areas. Firstly, they must handle and counsel delicate and sensitive issues among the home cell units. They will consecrate babies and officiate weddings, funerals, and anniversary services. Thirdly, they are to preside over Sunday morning services, speak on numerous Sunday night services, conduct dawn prayer meetings, and lead Friday all-night prayer meetings.[47]

Critical Elements of a Home Cell Group Meeting

This section discusses several vital components of cell group meetings. The first is prayer. The members are committed to prayer, especially for each other's needs. They include prayers for healing and financial provision. Through prayer, they practice their love, care, and concern for cell group members. Prayer is also offered for the salvation of members new to the group and the Christian faith. For certain critical matters, the leader and members even pray with fasting.[48] Testimonies of the answered prayers are regularly shared in the cell group meeting. This is "a practice which builds even greater faith as cell unit members turn their need-directed prayer to attend others." A couple once shared a moving testimony with their cell group. Due to constant clashes in their marriage life, they considered divorce. Upon learning of this challenge, the cell leader invited them to her

45. Hurston, *Growing the World's Largest Church*, 76.
46. Hurston, *Growing the World's Largest Church*, 76.
47. Hurston and Hurston, *Caught in the Web*, 38.
48. Hurston, *Growing the World's Largest Church*, 93.

home for prayer, but they rebuffed her. However, when the invitation was offered the second time, they accepted. Through their prayer and counsel, the couple experienced healing of their wounded relationship. Soon after, they became husband-wife leader teams over a home cell group.[49]

The cell meeting's second and most crucial element is teaching the word of God for daily Christian life and witness. The church has produced a series of seven study guides for home cell groups. This seven-year curriculum provides a systematic study of the Bible. The content is based on over four hundred expository sermons of Cho's primarily delivered in Wednesday evening services. Each lesson centers on one key topic of Christian life based on a scriptural passage. The layout for the weekly study guide lesson is as follows:

> Today's Scripture: This is the key text for the lesson. The group reads this part of the scripture out loud collectively.
>
> Memory Verse: As the core of the lesson, the group reads this scripture aloud in one voice a few times.
>
> Leading questions: Commonly, the leader invites a few initial questions that surfaced from reading "today's scripture."
>
> Today's Message: "Two to three pages in length, this pre-published note explains the week's topic. In most groups, the members read this note's paragraphs aloud until the entire message has been read." Then, the leader highlights essential points of the passage, occasionally interjecting personal illustrations.
>
> Closing Questions: The leader invites final comments and questions as he or she brings the "material from the lesson together."
>
> Applications: The lesson concludes with a few suggested applications to everyday life.[50]

The last element of the cell meetings is fellowship. The members freely share personal and family affairs with other members, often over refreshments. This enhances the unity in the body of Christ.[51] The whole process of the cell group meeting contributes to the harmony of the church. This harmony is based on a firm foundation: truth, dynamic faith, spiritual vitality, care for each other's needs, and compliance with leadership. The

49. Hurston and Hurston, *Caught in the Web*, 49–50.

50. Hurston, *Growing the World's Largest Church*, 94.

51. Hurston, *Growing the World's Largest Church*, 95.

members are constantly taught to exercise their faith through prayer for others. This vibrant harmony draws the members to spiritual growth in a "Christ-centered and Spirit-led" atmosphere. It further strengthens the members' faith and their dedication to Christ.[52]

CONCLUDING REMARKS

As discussed in this study, Confucianism has pervaded Korean society, especially in shaping values and social structures. The place of women has been a stark reminder of this philosophical system against gender equality.

In March 2017, the Ministry of Family and Women's Affairs reported that Korea ranks 142nd out of 193 nations in the index of women ministers. Although economically developed, the nation's progress in gender equality appears among underdeveloped or developing countries. Once with a woman president, it was counted among the nations such as England, Germany, Italy, the Netherlands, Spain, and France, whose prime ministers were women. However, it appears to be an exception in Korea rather than a norm. The newly elected president, Jae-in Moon, vowed to achieve a gender balance in his cabinet drastically. It is a clear sign of his awareness of the deeply rooted gender bias in Korea.[53]

However, the "image of women" in Asia, including Korea, has been improving in most societies, excluding several Muslim countries. Astonishingly, women today can work in conspicuous places and occupations once exclusively available only to men. However, what we experience in current times was unimagined in earlier years. The recent decision of the Saudi prince to allow women to drive is a case in point.[54]

In this general context, the cell group system of Yoido Full Gospel Church was revolutionary. When Cho made the final decision to appoint women leaders for the cell groups, some women also objected to the decision. This indicates how deeply ingrained the gender-biased value system was. Only the deep sense of God's vision gave Cho the necessary perseverance and persuasion. He sustained this countercultural system through the careful training of the leaders. The church carefully maintained the qualifications of these leaders. They occupied Cho's ministry priority as the

52. Hurston and Hurston, *Caught in the Web*, 57–58.

53. Dong-won Lee and Ju-ha Kim, *MBN News* broadcast, June 1, 2017.

54. Ma, "Changing Images,"203–14. See also Ma, "Role of Christian Women in the Global South," 194–206.

backbone of his church structure. As a result, the church grew dynamically and vibrantly in its spiritual life and numerical growth. After decades of experience, the system has proven to be genuinely empowering. Many churches throughout the world have adopted the cell-group system with necessary modifications. And in most cases, pastoral care has improved, as has church growth. Like in many social contexts, Korea has defied the long-established gender-bias system.

5

Touching the Lives of People Through the Holistic Mission Work of Mark and Huldah Buntain in Calcutta, India

THE MISSION WORK OF Mark Buntain and his wife, Huldah, started in Calcutta, India 1954. They accepted an invitation from the Foreign Missions Department of the Assemblies of God in the United States to go there for a year of evangelistic services. They stayed in Calcutta very much longer! Mark continued working until he died in 1989. And more than sixty years later, Huldah was still on the job. She decided not to stop after the death of her husband.[1]

In August 1954, the Buntains arrived in England; they discovered that the ship they were to travel on to India was not going! They had no choice but to stay in London, where they found lodging at a missionary guesthouse until they could arrange passage on another ship. Mark made a considerable effort, traveling daily to the Thomas Cook Travel Agents in downtown London to find out when they could book a passage on an alternative ship to Calcutta. However, the situation initially looked impossible. While they were in London, Mark had a chance to speak in some churches. Several days later, they received the good news that the SS *Orangie*, a Dutch passenger ship, was going to Ceylon, now Sri Lanka.[2]

The Buntains were pleased to learn that the ship's accommodations were either first or second class—nothing lower. Fortunately, the Missions Department approved their journey, and they purchased tickets. The

1. Buntain, *Pathway to the Impossible*, 11.
2. Buntain, "Fifty Years in Calcutta," 1.

conditions on the ship were decent and pleasing. After a long journey, the ship reached Colombo, Ceylon, on a Sunday morning in late September. A missionary couple, Harold and Beatrice Cole, were waiting and warmly welcomed them. However, the Buntains still had to find a ship or a freighter to go to Calcutta. While in Colombo, they received a telegram from Noel Perkin, the Foreign Missions director of the Assemblies of God. It read, "Proceed to Calcutta until further notice, letter awaiting there." They wondered what he meant by "further notice." Finally, they found the SS *The City of Madras*, a freighter with passenger cabins, was going to Calcutta. After a three-month journey on two ships, Mark and Huldah finally arrived in Calcutta and settled among treacherous surroundings on the Hooghly River.[3]

The Buntains arrived in India during difficult trials when many missionaries left to return to their home country in misery and desolation. Fellow missionaries were saying that mission work in India had become unbearable. Already a severely overcrowded city, Calcutta was occupied by "millions of refugees." Trade and airlines were withdrawing from this once-lively city, and it was becoming a place of total desperation. However, with conviction, passion, and firmness, the Buntains rejected the idea of being discouraged and giving up.[4] They started their work with a goal and deep commitment to reach Calcutta for Christ and to transform people's lives. After living there for a short while, they soon realized that the city had no hope for disabled children, the hurting and the hungry, and many other groups.[5] Knowing that parents had abandoned countless street children, they started a feeding program, and some years later, they opened a school and a hospital. Gradually, other ministries were established to meet people's needs and to provide hope. This article delineates their significant works and the works that continue now, many years after Mark and Huldah Buntain's deaths.

THE LIVING ENVIRONMENT IN CALCUTTA

When the Buntains entered the city by freighter, they noticed many surprising items floating on the murky Hooghly River, from trash to deceased animals. People were bathing in the water along the shores, and the Buntains

3. Buntain, *Pathway to the Impossible*, 11.
4. Buntain, *Pathway to the Impossible*, 12.
5. Valimont, "Calcutta Mercy Ministries Overview."

were shocked to see such abject poverty on every hand.[6] Warm breezes blew in their faces, but with each breath, they had to swallow thick and unpleasant pollutants that were in the air. The city was overflowing with illnesses and starvation, and people stumbled through "the last weeks of their lives. They were too frail to fight, yet too hard to die." They called for help, but no one responded; too many were there.[7] The muddy water looked like dirt flowing down an extensive drain, with dead dogs, cows, and even the parts of a human skeleton shockingly visible. Naked natives were washing in the water. Other people assembled on the banks, making Huldah think of "Tom Sawyer and Huckleberry Finn and the Mississippi Queen; then she realized the two settings had nothing in common."[8]

As they went through the crowd, children grabbed at their ankles and pleaded for a coin or morsel of food. Many of them were thin, frail, and malformed. Their eyes appeared like those of supercilious owls, looking at the Buntains as if they were magnificent deities coming to rescue them from the brutalities of their world.[9]

Huldah further described their new home as follows:

> Calcutta is a desperate city. Calcutta is the home of 18 million people, four miles wide and nine miles long. Eighty percent of the city is slums. There are 1,000 people at every toilet and 5,000 at every drinking fountain. Clapboard hovels, street vendors, beggars, half-naked children, and an estimated 40,000 human rickshaws fill the roads. Cows venerated as sacred monopolize the streets, forcing taxis and pedestrians from their path. Packs of dogs fight for scraps of food. Homeless men, women, and children lie on mats positioned in alleys and on patches of open pavement. Many are embroiled in a daily quest for survival, grown men jostling in line for a job that may pay 10 rupees a day (30 U.S. cents).[10]

The Buntains further mentioned that disease was rampant throughout the city: epidemics were impartial, snuffing out the lives of young and old. "Cholera, typhoid, tetanus, and more keep hospitals and mortuaries busy."[11] However, the population also included people who had sufficient food to

6. Buntain, *Treasures in Heaven*, 79.
7. Wead, *Compassionate Touch*, 8–10.
8. Buntain, *Treasures in Heaven*, 108.
9. Donaldson and Dobson, *Huldah Buntain*, 22.
10. Buntain, *Treasures in Heaven*, 21.
11. Buntain, *Treasures in Heaven*, 22.

eat. These women were beautifully dressed; some were good-looking young men with "mustaches and western shoes." Some were hugely affluent, even millionaires.[12] However, most people in the city were desperately struggling for their daily survival.

THE IMPETUS OF INVOLVEMENT IN DIVERSE SOCIAL MINISTRIES

Once, soon after they arrived in Calcutta, the Buntains were having a church worship service when a beggar appeared and shouted, "Preacher, feed our bellies, and then tell us there is a God."

The beggar's saying had stricken his heart, as the Buntains witnessed children who starved to death, and they learned that "millions of children in Calcutta live and die in the filth of poverty." This stark reality spoke deeply to the Buntains and moved them to begin a feeding program serving over sixty thousand meals a week through numerous serving posts.[13]

One day in school, Mark Buntain faced a critical situation as a girl collapsed in the classroom. He had to rush the child to the hospital. Still, he was disheartened to discover that the local hospital was overcrowded, and no medical staff could respond to this emergency quickly. This incident prompted him to begin to offer what he could in the way of medical care and food for children, besides providing for their educational needs. Eventually, Mark constructed a hospital in 1977, which offered free health care services to countless people, adults and children, suffering from various diseases.[14]

Such heart-wrenching personal experiences inspired the Buntains to engage in one social ministry after another. They strongly desired to provide people with good health care, adequate education, and a hopeful life overall. Aside from these experiences, the Buntains had compassionate hearts and love for the people. Huldah once described Mark's passion for helping for the sake of the Gospel: "With a tear-stained face, Mark looked at me and said, 'Huldah, there are hundreds of villages across these mountains. We don't have a gospel work in Darjeeling or in any of these villages, which cover hundreds of miles across the Himalayan Mountains.'"[15]

12. Wead, *Compassionate Touch*, 8–10.

13. Wead, *Compassionate Touch*, 8–10.

14. Wead, *Compassionate Touch*, 8–10.

15. Buntain, *Treasures in Heaven*, 48.

Starting a Feeding Ministry

Shortly after the Buntains settled down in Calcutta, they discovered that many street children had no proper name; they were referred to as "the one with measles" or "the kid with smallpox." Some died from starvation; others succumbed to bacterial and viral attacks. Because of malnutrition, their bodies had no strength to resist. "These dead lie with a puzzled look on their faces while some adult, a handkerchief gripped to nose and mouth, determines what happened." After encountering numerous people daily suffering from little or no food, the Buntains started a feeding ministry. At first, the numbers were small, but they kept on growing and continued to this day. The Calcutta Street Feeding Program provides food for many, including schoolchildren. The food is taken to various stations within a forty-five-minute range of Calcutta. Though the city has developed in multiple ways because of the influence of technology, the poor have seemed to increase, for floods of people are coming in from other cities looking for work and places to live. "The feeding lines continue to expand as thousands of families live on the streets and depend on these daily meals. One million children are estimated to live on the streets in Calcutta." For twenty-five thousand schoolchildren daily, it is the only meal they will have the whole day.[16]

Feeding huge numbers of people daily requires considerable finances. The Buntains frequently encountered financial challenges because of growth in numbers. The senior accountants occasionally say, "The feeding program account only has money for a couple more days to feed the children." Mark would take Huldah's hands and offer prayer on hearing this news. In such cases, he seemed always to receive the assurance that God knew about the financial difficulties and would not abandon them.[17] Even after her husband's death, Huldah continued to operate this ministry. She said, "When we needed money for our feeding programs and other charitable, compassionate ministries, I often thought we should consider downsizing these projects to take care of the daily operational expenses. At these times, however, when I was distressed over lack of finances and wondered where the money would come from, I would always be assured that God would take care of the problem, and miraculously, He always did."[18] The

16. Buntain, *Treasures in Heaven*, 48.
17. Buntain, *Treasures in Heaven*, 135.
18. Buntain, *Treasures in Heaven*, 135.

significant ministry of the feeding program has always continued. Many people rely extensively on this meal, although fundraising can sometimes be challenging.

Schools

The Buntains saw the urgent necessity of starting a school, for many children had no opportunity to go to school. A piece of land came to light that they wanted to purchase, but it belonged to a Muslim man who was very unwilling to sell. One day, Mark was called to visit this owner, who had been in the hospital for a long time with a critical illness. Mark held the man's hand and prayed for him as he sat by the bed. Shortly after that, news came that the man had died. The sons of the Muslim man, being highly superstitious, agreed to sell the land to Mark because he had been the last person to see their father alive. This was good news; however, he now faced the obstacle of raising the necessary funds to buy it.[19]

Because of financial need, Mark called for a prayer meeting one evening with his deacons. After the prayer meeting, he went home, filled with despair. Huldah welcomed him at the staircase to their flat and said, "You can end your prayers—the money is on its way!" Mark stared at Huldah, his face mixed with smiles and tears. Huldah explained, "I have a cable in my hand from your sister, Alice, saying that the funds are going to be sent to buy the property." Mark read the cable, then yelled, "Hallelujah!" Huldah gave him the whole story: "A layman in Alice's church in the States had asked her if anything was troubling her brother. Alice told the man about our financial crisis, and within days, he had wired what was needed to purchase the land. For Mark and me, it was as if God, through this miracle, repeated his vow never to forsake us. In response, all we could do was wrap our arms around one another and sigh a prayer of thanksgiving and relief into the other's ear."[20]

Building the primary school on this property went ahead. Mark found a dear "Indian-born female," Mrs. Shaw, attending an Assemblies of God church with considerable educational skills and experience and hired her as principal to manage the entire educational program. Mark sent out over five hundred invitations when they were preparing to open the school. However, as the dedication drew near, there was a political uprising in the

19. Buntain, *Treasures in Heaven*, 153.

20. Buntain, *Treasures in Heaven*, 153–54.

city, much like the campus unrest that swept through the United States in the 1960s. These events kept all but a few from attending the dedication, which was in January 1964. To everyone's amazement, two hundred students were enrolled shortly after the dedication.[21]

At this point, it seemed the enemy launched an all-out attack. Mark was stricken with pneumonia and needed to be hospitalized. At the same time, their daughter, Bonnie, "had a near-fatal bout with a high fever that turned into tropical measles." At the same time, catastrophic floods nearly overwhelmed the entire city, leaving thousands destitute and starving. The church fed a myriad of refugees. Because of blocked drains, it took weeks for the water to recede.[22]

Several years later, in 1979, Mark's long dream of setting up a nursing school came true. It was combined with the Calcutta Mercy Hospital. An advertisement at the time read, "The School of Nursing offers a two-year program, as well as a ten-month Diploma in Institutional Nursing Administration and Education and a three-year program in General Nursing and Midwifery."[23] It aimed to educate young women from needy backgrounds searching for a better future for themselves and their families. It was set up with specialized teaching staff and services to prepare graduates for healthcare vocations thoroughly. The school grew to the point where some twenty-five new students enroll yearly.[24] Graduates of the nursing programs find jobs at Calcutta Mercy Hospital or have places in Mercy Clinics.[25] In 2008, nursing school became a college degree program, which expanded the possibilities for graduates.[26]

After that, the first primary school succeeded in 1964, and almost every year after that, additional schools were set up. Eventually, the Buntains opened slightly over one hundred schools in Calcutta and nearby suburbs.[27] They also opened Bible colleges that trained hundreds of ministers.[28]

The Buntains also helped Calcutta Blind School as partners in home life, schooling, and medical care for underprivileged children struggling

21. Buntain, *Treasures in Heaven*, 156.
22. Buntain, *Treasures in Heaven*, 153–54.
23. Buntain, *Treasures in Heaven*, 123.
24. Buntain, *Treasures in Heaven*, 129–30.
25. Buntain Foundation, "About Us," 1.
26. Buntain Foundation, "About Us, 1.
27. Assembly of God Church Kolkata, "Our History."
28. Buntain, *Pathway to the Impossible*, 2.

with damage to their eyesight. Countless families in India could not pay for medical care for their blind children. In some cases, because parents believed that their child's deficiency was a curse on the family, they neglected or even deserted the child.[29]

Calcutta Mercy Ministries' dream is to grow yearly and assist more destitute people in different cities with further services. In 2015, a new College of Nursing facility opened. Its vision includes:

> Improving health care in hospitals to meet India's current shortage of 1.1 million nurses. At the request of the Indian Nursing Council, Calcutta Mercy Ministries is constructing a new College of Nursing facility that will exist in addition to the School of Nursing. Offering a higher degree in the nursing profession, nurses can expand their knowledge within specific medical fields and fill specialized roles that hospitals are currently lacking.[30]

Establishing a Hospital

Over their years of service in Calcutta, the Buntains witnessed countless people die because of insufficient medical care. As noted above, when Mark dealt with the girl who suddenly collapsed in her classroom, it gave him a burden for establishing a hospital. In 1971, they began a small health facility at the back of their Royd Street School. It began with one big room and six patient beds and with a few volunteer nurses and doctors. Mark and Huldah were grateful to God for the "development of medical and surgical procedures and personnel" and other necessary work on this facility.[31]

This small medical center constantly expanded, indicating that a larger facility was needed. They enlarged the capacity to sixteen beds, but it was soon inadequate to handle the demand. This hospital was very active in neighborhood programs of sickness prevention, which included free vaccinations and "basic medical care to schoolchildren, as well as to hundreds of people who would line up for treatment each day." The Buntains longed to construct a more significant medical center to provide God's care for bodily and spiritual needs. For days and weeks, Mark kept reminding himself of what happened with the child who collapsed in the classroom and with people having to share beds in congested local hospitals. He never lost hope

29. Valimont, "Calcutta Mercy Ministries Overview."

30. Valimont, "Calcutta Mercy Ministries Overview."

31. Buntain, *Treasures in Heaven*, 110.

because God's will was to establish a medical facility in Calcutta that could serve the poor.[32]

One day, Mark came home excitedly, saying he had discovered land suitable for a hospital on the central street of Calcutta. Huldah could not believe this news because they had searched for days and could not find anything in their current church, school, or small hospital neighborhood. She was astonished when Mark enthusiastically shared with her the property he discovered: a large "old British cemetery four blocks square that had not been used in over a hundred years." Since there were no tombs there, it was used by a sports club as a soccer field. Mark planned to meet with the cemetery Burial Board for assistance. After many hours of consultation with the board and its committees, they finally agreed to draw up an agreement for the Buntain's mission to purchase the land.[33]

The initial building permit that they received was for the hospital. However, Mark needed help to raise adequate funds for the initial groundwork. When they started digging, the contractors ran into water they did not expect; the more they dug, the more water came out. Huldah recalled her thrilling experience:

> I was very concerned as the water appeared like a large lake, and I knew we did not have money to fund the necessary pilings required for such a huge building. Mark gathered some of our pastors and staff together and said, "This is an attack of the enemy. We have to pray that God will work another miracle." I wondered what miracle Mark was talking about. When Mark took a little Bible out of his pocket, I knew something miraculous was going to happen. Mark then asked the contractors for a rope, which he tied around the Bible, and told everyone to join hands and believe God for a miracle. . . . He dropped the Bible down into the water, asked everyone to pray, and in a loud voice commanded the water to recede into the ground.[34]

Huldah could hardly believe her eyes. Amazingly, the water gradually withdrew back into the ground. The workers' eyes were "as big as saucers." They shouted, "Where did the water go?" In a calm voice, Mark whispered, "God took care of the situation." The workers were astonished.[35]

32. Buntain, *Treasures in Heaven*, 111.
33. Buntain, *Treasures in Heaven*, 112.
34. Buntain, *Treasures in Heaven*, 112–13.
35. Buntain, *Treasures in Heaven*, 113.

In 1977, after the building was finally finished and outfitted, the hospital began providing medical services for needy men, women, and children of Calcutta. Calcutta Mercy Hospital is a 6-story facility with 173 beds and 30 multi-specialty departments. Serving over one hundred thousand patients a year, forty thousand are treated free of charge, irrespective of their caste, creed, or religion. Ongoing programs provide free medical services to children suffering from blindness, cleft lips or palates, thalassemia, and leukemia.[36]

Besides operating the hospital, Calcutta Mercy Ministries operates eighteen Mercy Clinics and aims to open twenty-two more clinics. Daily, doctors and nurses travel from Calcutta Mercy Hospital to satellite clinics, giving free health care to communities around the countryside. Underprivileged families living in rural villages without money to travel to the city can quickly get medical care through Mercy Clinics. Calcutta Mercy Ministries works yearly to provide new areas with sympathetic, necessary "end-to-end" care. Nurses obtain advanced medical knowledge through the New College of Nursing facility. Self-sufficiency is vital, as hospital programs strive to make the yearly income cover running expenses, as 40 percent of the hospital's services are free to poor people.

Calcutta Mercy Hospital and its partners have dedicated much time to Sonagachi, the red-light district of Calcutta. Sonagachi is home to over ten thousand prostitutes living within a one-mile radius. Mercy Ministries has supported free medical clinics in the area, striving to provide a safe place where women and their children can receive much-needed medical care.[37]

The hospital continually makes significant strides in adding more facilities, developing into one of Calcutta's top medical centers. For instance, recently, the Mark Buntain Cardiac Unit was dedicated.[38] Mother Teresa, who lived in Calcutta and worked directly on some projects with the Buntains, suffered from heart disease, which was the cause of her death. After Mother Teresa's death, Huldah and Jim Long, her son-in-law who is a medical doctor and plays a vital role in the hospital, along with a few others, strongly felt that it was essential to equip the hospital with a heart unit, which was a desire that Mark Buntain shared with Mother Teresa. It was miraculously provided. "It was not long after that our good friend Bob

36. Buntain, *Treasures in Heaven*, 114.

37. Valimont, "Calcutta Mercy Ministries Overview." See also Wead, *Compassionate Touch*, 9.

38. Donaldson and Dobson, *Huldah Buntain*, 81.

Pagett, who founded Assist International to furnish hospitals with equipment in Third World countries, knew of our need. He contacted us with the wonderful news that a hospital in California was donating a complete Cardiac Care Unit, which included everything we needed."[39]

When sick people who could not go to a hospital because they could not pay medical bills came to the Buntains and asked for help, their wish was granted without hesitation. Those seriously ill, so weak that even a doctor could not tell whether they would survive an operation, were treated. The Buntains earnestly prayed for divine intervention in such critical conditions. In many cases, many nonbelievers who found healing through medical care and the Buntains' love for them expressed their wish to attend church.

Establishing Calcutta Mercy Ministries

After Mark Buntain died in 1989 and was buried in Calcutta, Huldah struggled with whether she would keep on with the mission work. Thinking of continuing the ministries with no husband was overwhelming; the undertaking was a huge responsibility, and the needs seemed more incredible than ever. For a woman like Huldah in her early sixties at the time, to go forward seemed to make no sense. She was convinced, however, that God held her hand and was leading her down a path to the impossible. After much prayer, she sensed God's confirmation of her call to continue the work. In fact, in a corner of her heart, she desired to finish her job, return to the United States, and live close to her daughter, Bonnie, and Bonnie's family. In 2005, however, Huldah and Bonnie founded Calcutta Mercy Ministries to support the ongoing ministry in India. The surprising fact is that not only was Huldah maintaining the existing ministries, but her care for needy people was expanding![40]

Other Ministries

Under the umbrella organization Transformation India Movement (TIM) more than 150 villages have been adopted in the nearby state of Bihar. According to its website, TIM gives every village two hundred Bibles and

39. Donaldson and Dobson, *Huldah Buntain*, 137.

40. Valimont, "Calcutta Mercy Ministries Overview."

hymnals for new believers, a much-needed clean-water drinking well for the village, ongoing literacy training, a one-time medical clinic/VBS program, a bike for the church planter, and the Jesus Film or a Christian movie.[41] This program, called Adopt-A-Village, is undertaken by qualified church planters of TIM and aims to plant churches. These Adopt-A-Village ministries are for communities without any Christian presence. Through this ministry, hundreds of churches in different villages have been started. It also provides "community development programs to unreached areas of rural India."[42]

From its modest beginning, Calcutta Mercy Ministries has expanded to include even more programs. The number of churches planted has reached eight hundred. In addition, there are several Bible colleges and a teacher's college. Huldah supervised them all through her regular visits. Such involvement allowed her to stay at home only three or four months a year. The other months, she traveled and visited various places in India and worldwide, overseeing ministries in eleven Indian states, comprising 230 million people until she died in 2021. Thirty thousand children from these areas are in Mission of Mercy schools.[43]

EVALUATION OF THE BUNTAINS' MISSION WORK

The Buntains boldly started the holistic mission in Calcutta. Back in 1954, it was rather unusual for Pentecostal missionaries to be directly involved in social work; the more normal focus was church planting and evangelism, and only then did they gradually include social work based on the needs of local people. Historical records of the mission work of Elva Vanderbout in the Philippines (1947), for example, indicate that she was initially heavily involved in "power evangelism" in Northern Luzon and only later broadened out to include other social ministries such as an orphanage and a youth camp.[44] Numerous written records indicate that power demonstrations in healing and casting out demons have been a typical way of doing mission work for Pentecostals. The Buntains' priorities thus appear to be an exception to the established Pentecostal mission practice. However, they

41. "Transformation India Movement," 1–3.

42. Valimont, "Calcutta Mercy Ministries Overview."

43. "Transformation India Movement," 1–3.

44. Ma, *When the Spirit Meets the Spirits*, 83–85.

also shared the ultimate goal of evangelism, which led to the establishment of hundreds of churches.

Recently, Pentecostals have cultivated important mission programs to care for victims of societal unfairness.[45] Pentecostal missionaries and church leaders serving among the deprived and the poor commonly stress that the human person is the basis and reason for Christian missions.[46] That is, meeting the fundamental needs of life is a primary work.

Regarding holistic evangelism, we could say that it is to bring people to a saving knowledge of Christ and, second, to transform people's everyday lives. Such evangelism, which combines proclaiming the Gospel and doing social ministries, is far more effective for bringing transformation than just declaring the Gospel alone. The Buntains' holistic mission dealt with meeting people's felt needs and became a vehicle to transform people's lives in the deepest sense. In parallel with their tireless and lavish giving, their incarnational life demonstrated in diverse ministries touched people's hearts. Numerous unbelievers told of the Buntains' genuine love for Christ in books written by Huldah Buntain. One specific occasion displays how much Mark Buntain cared for a dying beggar.

> A crippled beggar sat at our Mission gate. Our workers would bring him food from the feeding program across the street. One day, we noticed that the old beggar was very sick. He was lying down and almost unconscious. Immediately, Mark took him to our hospital. The doctors said, "Pastor, you have brought us in a dead man." Mark replied, "Yes, I know, but I want him to die between clean sheets and tell him that Jesus loves him." After he was put in one of our hospital beds, Mark leaned down and said, "Do you know Jesus?" He suddenly gained consciousness, looked up in Mark's face, and said, "Are you Jesus?" Mark said, "No, I am not Jesus, but I want you to know that He loves you and wants to take you to a better place called heaven." . . . He prayed the sinner's prayer, closed his eyes with a smile on his face, and went to be with Jesus.[47]

A similar story of a missionary's Christlike life also demonstrates this effect. John Bosco (1815–88), founder of the Salesians (who in 1934 opened St. Anthony's College in Shillong, India), and his colleagues were very well received because of their impact on unbelievers through their

45. Ma and Ma, *Mission in the Spirit*, 279.

46. Alvarez, "Pentecostals, Society, and Christian Mission in Latin America," 302.

47. Ma, *When the Spirit Meets the Spirits*, 204.

lives. "As the people saw how John Bosco and his Christian colleagues and friends were involved with their problems, the worst drunkards in the factory and some residents of the slums became Christians." Then in a small room in the slum area, Bosco and his partners taught Christian workers, and their family members based on their practical skills. These people who were ministered to by Bosco gave him their feedback: "By what you have done, you have painted us a portrait of Jesus."[48] Whether it is proclaiming the Gospel or doing social work, the incarnational life of Gospel bearers is significant in transforming people's lives. It should be one of the chief aims of cross-cultural missionaries.

CONCLUDING REMARKS

This chapter highlights the Buntains' dedicated and committed mission service in Calcutta, although we have had to be very selective in what was covered. It is interesting to consider their decision to go to Calcutta, initially for only one year, which stretched to over sixty years. God put them there to perform his will and purpose for the people of Calcutta. The Buntains entered a new horizon of ministries that they never anticipated: social works of opening various schools, engaging in feeding programs, running a hospital, and many others. Countless children received significant benefits from their medical services, not to mention schooling and being fed. Likewise, adults benefited through a variety of generous social services. Such services played an important role in bringing people to the knowledge of Jesus Christ and in enabling them to experience transformation in their lives.

Mark and Huldah Buntain were unsparing in their sacrifices. On one occasion, Mark suffered from draining fatigue and eventually was confined in a hospital. A few days later, a doctor pressed Huldah, saying, "I'm afraid your husband is suffering from severe fatigue, and unless he learns to rest, he's not going to live long. We've taken away his Bible and preaching tapes. He has a seventy-year-old body. He's not sleeping without sedatives, and we can't get him to eat. Please, take him back to Canada or the United States."[49]

The Buntains were making unceasing efforts, including fundraising, to set up ministries they had been running. His physical weakness affected his heart and mind. However, Huldah's abundant faith cheered him up, simply

48. McAlpine, *By Word, Work, and Wonder*, 103.

49. Buntain, *Treasures in Heaven*, 150.

by her saying, "Don't give up!"[50] They were partners not only in ministry but also in their spiritual lives. The Buntains were more than unselfish in giving to those in need. Their sympathy for the poor and the deprived never declined; instead, it increased—they fed more people as the years went by. What has been the crucial element at the center of all their ministries? It is Christ's love they had in their hearts. Parents of sick children who came to them frequently asked, "Why do you do this, and why do you love our children?"[51] The Buntains believed there is no better way of providing them with the love and compassion of Christ than meeting their needs through medical care, providing food, and educating them.

Such an approach certainly brings to mind Matt 25:35–40, which spells out very clearly the significance of what the Buntains had done: "For I was hungry, and you gave me something to eat, I was thirsty and you gave me something to drink, I was a stranger, and you invited me in, I needed clothes, and you clothed me. . . . LORD, when did we see you hungry and feed you, or thirsty and give you something to drink? . . . I tell you the truth, whatever you did for one of the least of these brothers of mine, you did for me."

50. Buntain, *Treasures in Heaven*, 151.

51. Buntain, *Treasures in Heaven*, 129.

6

Asian Women and Pentecostal Ministry

According to Jewish custom, men celebrated the Feast of Pentecost only. However, both men and women experienced the outpouring of the Holy Spirit on that day.[1] Peter's preaching from the prophet Joel was that "sons and daughters" would prophesy,[2] and this has since been a critical encouragement for women to enter Christian ministry. This was particularly true for those with roots in the nineteenth-century Holiness movement.[3] Pentecostals have believed strongly in the notion of the call of God. Unmarried and married women have worked in various ministry settings primarily to fulfill their sense of being called. They are church planters, preachers, counselors, teachers, and doctors in far-off corners. Their God-given gifts and empowerment are used for particular purposes and tasks, and this sense of divine call was more significant than limitations set by institutions and mission organizations.

In local ministry settings, women are also used effectively. Some women have enormously influenced churches, schools, and, in Korea, prayer mountains. Women work hard with their distinctive spiritual gifts and strong commitment. However, Asian women, in general, have been deprived of their calling and their potential because their culture has commonly failed to recognize women's leadership qualities and capabilities, both in society and in the church. Although there are some improvements

1. Acts 1:14–15; 2:1.
2. Cavaness, "God Calling," 49–62.
3. Cundall, *Judges and Ruth*, 88.

in women's roles in various ways due to the influence of globalization, full recognition is still minimal.

In this section, I will discuss several critical issues for women in Asia, such as women's involvement in the mission field and their ministry in the local setting.

WOMEN OF THE BIBLE IN MINISTRY

Deborah is an outstanding female leader in the Old Testament. Judges 4:1–15 notes a story of conquest through the leadership of Deborah. This narrative is about Israel in combat with Canaan. They are understood to be a sturdy nation with a strong military.[4] The Israelites were, for an extended period, brutally exploited by the Canaanites. Unbearable persecution from the Canaanites finally caused the Israelites to implore the help of God (4:1–3). The brave judge Deborah, the woman who led Israel during this time, was determined to do something by battling with Canaan. Deborah commanded Barak, son of Abinoam, to get ten thousand men of Naphtali and Zebulun and direct them to Mount Tabor. A fascinating fact in this description is the human plot incorporated into God's strategy (4:7). Deborah said, from what she heard from God, "I will lure Sisera, the commander of Jabin's army, with his chariots and his troops to the Kishon River and give him into your hands." Deborah revealed her tremendous faith, bravery, and wits, enabling Barak to succeed. She ascertained for herself and Barak the victory of God in her nation.[5] Deborah ordered Barak, "Go! This is the day the LORD has given Sisera into your hands; has not the LORD gone ahead of you?" As Deborah prophesied, God routed Sisera, the commander of Jabin's army of Canaan, and all his chariots and army. Sisera deserted his chariot and darted away on foot (4:14–15). Deborah's leadership was recognized in the battle with Canaan. Her wisdom was used for the battle and to bring about the victory. Indeed, God was with his people and fought for them.

In the New Testament, other women, who did not necessarily occupy prominent positions, were magnificently used by God to complete his purpose. Women who followed the Lord during his ministry witnessed the final moments of his death. Matthew 27:55 records the account of women who followed Jesus from Galilee to care for his needs: they are Mary Magdalene,

4. Cundall, *Judges and Ruth*, 88.

5. Ma, *When the Spirit Meets the Spirits*, 166.

Mary the mother of James and Joses, and the mother of Zebedee (Matt 27:56). These women never left the tomb where the body of Jesus was placed. This shows their heart and love for the Lord, even against the fear of cultural expectations and the guards. Matthew 28:5–7 notes, "The angel said to the women, 'Do not be afraid, for I know that you are looking for Jesus, who was crucified. He is not here; he has risen, as he said.'" Then, the angel commissioned the women to move promptly to Galilee and report to the disciples (28:7), who feared that the Lord had not risen from the dead. With great joy, the women went on their way to Galilee, and they encountered Jesus. He gave them the same order as the angel, to go to Galilee and tell his disciples that he would appear to them (28:10).

These women became the messengers who brought the good news of the resurrection of Jesus to the disciples. Although the women never spent much time with Christ, they proved that their faith in him was much stronger than that of the disciples, and they were used amazingly in the final moments.

WOMEN'S ISSUES IN ASIA

I will highlight a few of the issues in this section.

The Degeneration of Women

In some countries in Asia, women are dehumanized. Although women are offered more opportunities in society and are better treated in the new century, the traditional attitude toward women persists. Women are not adequately considered and recognized for their societal and church roles. Many decades ago, women were victims of government, military, and societal oppression. One particular woman's organization, the Christian Conference of Asia Women's Concerns Consultation, held a conference in Ginowan Seminar House (also known as The Ecumenical Peach Centre), Okinawa, Japan, from June 19–25, 1992, under the watchwords "Called to Be Peacemakers." Participants came from Korea, Japan, Taiwan, Philippines, Hong Kong, Sri Lanka, Australia, and Papua New Guinea.[6] From the many striking facts reported at this conference, I will here consider the

6. Hayes, "Sowing the Grains of Peace," 1.

"issue of the dehumanization of women" to present an overview of women in the past.[7]

Seventy percent of the world's thirteen million refugees were women at the time of the conference. Such cruel confinement in refugee camps destroys their humanity. This kind of treatment led women to kill their babies in Okinawa in World War II, which led to the suicide of Korean "comfort women" in Japan, which led, through poverty, to the sale and theft of women and children in the Philippines, Taiwan, Thailand, and other Asian countries; which leads to women being prostituted especially around military bases and for the entertainment of tourists, in many parts of the world; which leads to the perversion of children in military training; which leads to women taking up arms in Sri Lanka where they are encouraged to commit suicide if they are caught. This clearly shows that women were indeed the victims of war and were indeed heart-wounded.

How about in the current era? Are women any less the victims, and are they treated any better than before? My immediate response is a qualified "Yes." But being better treated does not necessarily mean being treated equally with men. I am not talking from a feminist activist's viewpoint but from the viewpoint of justice for all humanity. In Vietnam, girls have less chance to benefit from an education than boys. There are primary differences in the opportunities for boys and girls who finish primary school to proceed to government secondary schools. Places are usually rationed by examination, and frequently, the girls have lower chances due to their poor performance on the exam. The primary reason is that girls may spend far more time working for household resources than boys.[8]

In 1955, Malaysia formulated the Employment Act, which benefits workers.[9] This is the core legislation that governs the function of all "labor relations." Some areas apply equally to men and women, such as service contracts, salary, break time, working time, holidays, annual leave, sick leave, etc.[10] Certain aspects of this provision, however, are unfavorable to female workers. Against stipulations in the act, female employees are paid lower wages than male workers for doing equal labor. "Women in the private sector are subject to wage discrimination compared to their male

7. Hayes, "Sowing the Grains of Peace," 33.

8. McDonald, *Women in Development*, 43.

9. Ahmad, *Women in Malaysia*, 12.

10. Ahmad, *Women in Malaysia*, 12.

counterparts."[11] Today, Malaysian men and women, as well as international workers, are paid the same minimum salary. Additionally, gender discrimination is illegal. A policy has now been developed which ensures that Malaysian women are given growing opportunities to participate in the country's national growth in areas of the economy and work market, as well as better admission to education and health.[12]

In China, women encounter unfair treatment when seeking employment. A 1997 investigation, authorized by an official newspaper for students, discovered that female graduates from colleges and universities face far more rejection rates than male graduates in the labor market. Women accounted for 34 percent of the graduates in 1996. However, twenty-seven out of forty-two government organizations at a 1996 employment conference in Beijing refused to interview female candidates. According to the Beijing Graduate Employment Consulting Centre, "Discrimination against women is a social difficulty, which can only be resolved when social and economic standards have risen."[13]

Women have gradually moved into a better place and are treated better than in the 1940s. However, there needs to be more improvements in women's positions, opportunities, and recognition in society and churches.

Violence Against Women and Girls[14]

"The Universal Declaration of Human Rights" provides liberty for every individual—male or female—fundamental to human life.[15] For women, these rights have been violated in the following ways: sexual assault, sexual harassment, and verbal mistreatment intended to disgrace them. The use of a woman's body to sell cars and other goods makes objects of women. Moreover, scenes of rape and other violations against women are needlessly shown in films, soap operas, and comic books.[16]

Men in Korea are offered military service when they reach around the age of nineteen or twenty. Specific male characteristics are reshaped during military training. Confucianism's influence in Korean men's minds

11. Ahmad, *Women in Malaysia*, 12.
12. Ahmad, *Women in Malaysia*, 4.
13. Ahmad, *Women in the People's Republic of China*, 35.
14. Illo, *Women in the Philippines*, 16.
15. Jimenez-David et al., *Towards Our Own Image*, 6.
16. Jimenez-David et al., *Towards Our Own Image*, 16.

is another factor, particularly in valuing women. "Sowing the Grains of Peace" depicts the attitude of men in Korea. From an early age, men receive military training, and in adulthood, they join the army and continue to live in a militarized society. From there, they acquire militaristic values and ways of thinking, which become tied to the Confucian value system, which emphasizes the dominance of men over women. They regard women as objects, with low positions, as assistants or subdued ones. Assault and battery of wives, discriminatory treatment, low wages at work, human trafficking (kidnapping women for prostitution), sexual torture, and physical violence are committed by men who are deeply influenced by militarization.[17]

Some years ago, a policeman in Korea detained a female student and abused her sexually. In another incident, a group of policemen raped a woman. In 1980, a fresh military occurrence appeared, which was called the "35 policy." The policy aims to restrain people's awareness through sex, sports, and the screen. Information relating to the use of women in the "enjoyment industry" in South Korea demonstrates that 5 percent to 7.5 percent of the female populace (1,200,000–1,500,000) is drawn in. This statistic also includes the women who followed the locations of the US Army in Korea.[18]

The Philippine government's survey noted that, on average, one in every ten women has been beaten; a much smaller percentage has been pushed to engage in sex with someone. Some of the victims searched for places of help, such as the "Women's Crisis Centre," Lihok Pilipina in Cebu City and Metro Manila, and hospitals like the Philippine General Hospital.[19] It should be noted that physical and sexual exploitation is not only a problem of human rights in society but is also part of the economic issue. Women who work at night report incidences of broken bones or badly bruised wounds. They often hide the signs of their pain from fellow workers.[20]

Children are also victims of local violence. A survey shows that from 1991 to 1996, 8,355 cases of child maltreatment were reported to the Department of Social Welfare and Development.[21] All the victims of child abuse were girls, between ages eleven to seventeen years old. More than

17. Hayes, "Sowing the Grains of Peace," 13.

18. Hayes, "Sowing the Grains of Peace," 13.

19. Illo, *Women in the Philippines*, 17.

20. Illo, *Women in the Philippines*, 16–17.

21. UNICEF, "Over 370 Million Girls and Women Globally."

half of the girls had been sexually abused. Thus, the victims indicated or showed symptoms of sexually transmitted diseases (STDs).[22] Most incidents of child abuse occurred at home while the victims were alone and while parents were away for work. The majority of the perpetrators were found to be male relatives.[23]

A common form of violence affecting women is sexual abuse. They become prey to sexual exploitation by men. I have speculated on this issue and considered how long it will continue and if there are any possible ways to minimize sexual abuse.

Less Opportunity for Education

Philippine women are fortunate to have the benefit of education. At the national level, there are virtually no gender gaps in literacy and school attendance rates, although there are regional variations. For example, about 50 percent of children drop out before they reach the sixth grade. Among adults, female illiteracy dramatically exceeds male illiteracy. The illiteracy problem in Mindanao can be traced back to two factors with divergent gender effects: the peace and order problem, which has affected the school attendance of boys, and cultural prescriptions that inhibit the education of girls.[24]

As mentioned in the previous section, women in Vietnam have fewer educational opportunities. Poverty is one of the main reasons why women lose their chance at schooling. There is a considerable burden on needy families when sending their children to school. Furthermore, girls in poor families experience severe disadvantages. If parents are forced to take their children out of school due to financial difficulties, they will take the girls out first rather than the boys.[25]

According to a 1998 survey in China, female school enrolment at the primary, secondary, and higher education levels, as a proportion of entire enrollments from 1982 to 1996, showed a general increase in female enrollment. However, there is still a gap between male and female enrollment, which broadens as the education level increases.[26] In some Asian countries

22. UNICEF, "Over 370 Million Girls and Women Globally."
23. UNICEF, "Over 370 Million Girls and Women Globally."
24. Asian Development Bank, *Poverty in Viet Nam*, 28.
25. Asian Development Bank, *Poverty in Viet Nam*, 28.
26. Ahmad, *Women in the People's Republic of China*, 30.

such as Japan, Korea, Singapore, Malaysia, and Hong Kong, women may have a better chance of going on to higher education than women in Muslim countries who, unfortunately, have very little opportunity to experience higher education.

A FEW SELECTED ASIAN WOMEN IN PENTECOSTAL MINISTRY

Many Asian women have sincerely responded to a call from God. Below, I have described several outstanding women whose impact was enormous on the Pentecostal church and beyond.

Seenok Ahn

On August 22, 1924, the eldest of four brothers and sisters, Seenok Kim[27] was born in Pyongyang. She grew up attending a church close to her house even though neither of her parents was a Christian. She attended Teachers' College because she wanted to become a teacher like Pestalozzi, despite her parents' wishes for her to attend medical school. In 1942, she started working as a high school teacher after earning her degree from Teachers' College. Because of World War II, Koreans living under Japanese occupation rule endured a wretched existence throughout that period. She frequently went to the Pyongyang Orphanage with her students to support and soothe them. She first met her spouse, Ki Seuk Ahn, in that orphanage. Ahn put much effort into helping the orphans. Many people who had their belongings stolen flocked to the orphanage. He established a "Min-A-Dan," a relief organization, to feed and heal them as he could not feed them all. She frequently visited this orphanage to support his work. In the process, they developed feelings for one another, and October 1946 marked the couple's marriage. On June 25, 1950, early on a Sunday, the Korean War began. It was among the worst and most wretched wars in recorded history. Due to ideological differences, the Korean people—who shared the same ancestors, blood, and origin—fought against one another. It was the Ahns who fled North Korea. They encountered multiple perilous situations, yet amazingly, God delivered them each time. Many people, including parents, kids, siblings, relatives, and acquaintances, passed away. They established

27. Kim was her last name before marriage.

the In-Dong Presbyterian Church in Taejon as pioneers after relocating to the south.[28]

Educational Ministry

North Korea did not hold the Ahns back. They were in danger multiple times, yet amazingly, God delivered them each time. Numerous acquaintances died. Following their relocation to the south, they established the In-Dong Presbyterian Church in Taejon; later, the church's name was changed to Taejon Foursquare Gospel Church.[29]

In 1953, the Ahns assembled the refugees and started teaching them in a small, wood-framed hall partially destroyed, close to Taejon. That marked the start of Daesung Christian School. This little school soon expanded into six, employing four hundred teachers and serving over eight thousand students, turning it into one of Korea's leading private Christian high schools in Daejon City, South Korea.[30] The school held chapel services regularly, enabling students to hear the word of God and accept Christ into their hearts. Also, the schools incorporate a Bible subject in their curriculum, an indirect means of evangelism among the students. Many students who have graduated from the school have committed their lives to full-time ministry and mission work.[31]

While the school was being run, God opened a door for Ahn to receive theological training in the United States. This experience helped to broaden her perspective on educating young people. She studied the Bible and theology in Portland for three years. She visited Los Angeles as well. She met Rolf K. McPherson, the president of the International Church of the Foursquare Gospel. She earned a higher education degree and was an ordained minister of the Foursquare Church when she returned to Korea in 1970.[32]

28. Eim, "Amazing Ministry of Rev. Dr. Seen Ok Ahn," 1–2.
29. Eim, "Amazing Ministry of Rev. Dr. Seen Ok Ahn," 2.
30. Eim, "Pentecostalism and Public School," 3.
31. Eim, "Amazing Ministry of Rev. Dr. Seen Ok Ahn," 3.
32. Eim, "Pentecostalism and Public School," 1–22.

Other Significant Ministries

To prepare the young graduates of these schools to serve as missionary fighters in Southeast Asia, Ahn had a vision that they would get spiritual training while enrolled in the institutions. She decided to train them all in a single year. It was an intense four-day spiritual training program. The training places special emphasis on "conversion" for first-year students, "baptism with the Holy Spirit" for second-year students, and "the responsibility as a man and a woman of God in the society" for third-year students. Youth Mission Training (YMT) was what she called it. This training started on Friday afternoon and concluded on Sunday afternoon. There would be about ninety-nine lovingly trained adult staff members serving them. They never compelled them to perform tasks. Instead, every employee provided them with Christian love service. Good food, inspirational teachings, and the love of Christ are provided to all pupils. They feel a love they would never be able to feel anywhere else. By the time they completed the program, nearly all of them had come to know Jesus Christ as their Savior. After the program, their parents are also welcome. And many of them believe in Jesus Christ. Since 1989, almost sixteen thousand people had received training as of May 1999. Many of them decided to become missionaries in the future.[33]

Ahn did not limit herself to being involved in the educational arena but expanded into other works. She was involved in evangelism among prisoners for more than twenty years. She preached the gospel to various criminals and subsequently won many souls to Christ. Her boldness for Christ led her to inauspicious places like prisons where men were dominant, and she also presented the good news to them. Working together with the Holy Spirit, the results of her ministry were overwhelming.

Ahn also pioneered churches, growing rapidly in numbers to the point of being the most prominent church among the Foursquare churches in Korea. Her spiritual life was so remarkable that she committed to fasting for forty days when she was sixty. People around her were very concerned about her health, but she went through it well.[34] Ahn continues to exercise her spirituality in prayer and fasting, even to date.

33. Eim, "Amazing Ministry of Rev. Dr. Seen Ok Ahn," 9–10.

34. Ahn, *Fasting Prayer*, audio tapes.

Trinidad Seleky

Trinidad Seleky (Esperanza before marriage) was born November 6, 1922, in Pangasinan, Philippines. She was one of a few prominent women in Pentecostal churches. Seleky graduated from Bethel Bible College in 1948, from Northwest College in Kirkland, Washington, in 1962, and completed her master's degree at Fuller Theological Seminary. She was the first Filipino graduate from this seminary. Her most significant contribution was educating and training future Asian leaders at Asia Pacific Theological Seminary. In 1967, she joined the teaching staff and served for many years in its administration. Besides teaching courses in education at the seminary, she conducted seminars. She was involved in various ministries such as vacation Bible school, youth camps, children's crusades, Sunday school curriculum development, and training Christian education workers. She traveled throughout the Philippines, teaching and sharing her burden for the Christian education ministry.

Her other ministries involved: (1) Community outreach programs: She was actively engaged in community outreach initiatives, frequently emphasizing health, education, and community empowerment for impoverished areas. (2) Assistance for women and kids: She backed efforts to improve women's and children's well-being, such as those that offer resources and education to those in need. And (3) advocacy for social causes: Seleky advocated for social problems through her platform, using her prominence to draw attention to and support a range of humanitarian endeavors. Her involvement in social and humanitarian issues demonstrated a solid dedication to positively impacting society, even outside her professional career.[35]

From 1980 to 1987, Seleky served the Philippine General Council of the Assemblies of God as treasurer and national director of the Sunday School Department. She liaised between the seminary and the rest of the evangelical works in the Philippines. She also led the Philippine Association of Christian Education, which developed the doctor of education program. In May 1987, Seleky received a doctor of divinity from Southern California Theological Seminary. Her dedication to teaching and God's ministry is remarkable.[36]

35. Personal interview with Seleky.

36. Lou Gomez at Asia Pacific Theological Seminary provided the information.

Virgie Cruz

Virgie Cruz was a Filipino born on October 5, 1930, in Paete, Laguna, Philippines. Cruz ministered as an international evangelist and was the founding pastor of a large church in Manila. She conducted many evangelistic crusades in large cities within the country and overseas. The results were immense, in that hundreds gave their lives to Christ and further committed to his service. Her dynamic message, together with the work of the Holy Spirit, penetrated the people's hearts and made them repent. Cruz was used not only in evangelism but also in pastoral work. Her vibrant leadership caused church members to become involved in active evangelism. While the church grew, it also expanded its ministry into diverse realms: caring for the community, helping the poor, reaching young people, and so on. Cruz influenced and challenged numerous young people to engage in the gospel ministry during her pastoral work. Besides evangelistic crusades and preaching, she was also involved in other ministries.

Essential facets of her missionary efforts consist of the following:[37]

1. Evangelistic Crusades: Cruz planned and directed large evangelistic gatherings throughout the Philippines. These crusades sought to uplift people's spirits, spread the Christian message, and promote spiritual development.
2. Community Outreach: She frequently incorporated substantial community outreach initiatives into her crusades, such as offering aid and support to nearby towns. Programs about social services, education, and health may fall under this category.
3. Church Growth and Leadership: Cruz was instrumental in expanding and advancing numerous churches via her evangelistic endeavors. Congregations around the nation have grown and strengthened thanks to her guidance.
4. Media and Communication: Virgie Cruz used various media outlets to disseminate her message and broaden the scope of her evangelistic work. Digital media, television, and radio are all included in this.

37. Personal interview with Cruz.

Other Women

God has used countless Asian women. For instance, Susan Tang has been planting and pastoring churches in Sabah, Malaysia, for over twenty years. Her dedication to God's kingdom has resulted in many converts, churches, and countless pastors and evangelists. Another woman, Teo Kwee Keng, has pastored a thriving church in Batu Pahat, Malaysia, for fourteen years, pioneering at least four other churches in the area and serving at many preaching points.[38] Norma Lam has served as a female missionary in the Philippines from the same country, teaching at an international seminary for twelve years. While teaching at the seminary, she also extended herself to local mission work with Filipino missionaries Anita Swartz and Adeline Ladera, who have worked together in the Ministry Development Program of the seminary. The regular mission consists of evangelism, medical services, preaching, and teaching in mountain village churches. Her ministry extends to the Philippines, Cambodia, Indonesia, China, Malaysia (her home country), Singapore, and many other Asian countries. Numerous Asian women serve as cross-cultural missionaries: Nora Catipon, a single Filipino missionary, went to Cambodia to teach in the Bible School; another woman, Erlinda Reyes, has joined an international training ministry working with missionary staff from many other countries. In the 1960s, Maria Gomez in East Timor was called to service at a particular island where a prison stood and where various criminals were confined. She and her husband spent many years planting the seeds of the gospel by building churches and training young people. One night, when they had an evening service, the Holy Spirit fell upon the congregation, people confessed their sins, and remarkable healings occurred. Now, the whole island is called the Assemblies of God Island. Gomez is the current general superintendent in East Timor.[39]

In Singapore, from 1950 to 1960, Lula Baird, Lau To Chan, Sarah Johnson, and Jean Wagner were instrumental in establishing Grace Assembly. It is now a thriving church of nearly seventeen hundred parishioners.[40] It is noted,

38. Cavaness, "God Calling," 49–62.

39. Bill Snider, speaking at the Missions Emphasis Week at Asia Pacific Theological Seminary in 1997.

40. Abeysekera, *History of the Assemblies of God of Singapore*, 206–13.

> Women made up 26 percent of the list of the Assemblies of God-ordained and licensed ministers in Indonesia, 36 percent of the list in Malaysia, and 34 percent of the list in Singapore (totaling over 250 women). The Assemblies of God in the Philippines has a lot of women pastors and workers, and women make up about one-half (100) of the number of foreign missionaries being sent out from Singapore AG churches. The more than 130 AG Bible schools and one seminary in the Asia Pacific have large contingents of female students preparing for ministry.[41]

Asian women may have received encouragement from fellow female missionaries, as seen in the case of Elva Vanderbout. Also, Ruth Breusch was a missionary to India and greatly impacted local churches, while Naomi Dowdey founded and pastored the largest Assemblies of God church in Singapore.[42] Lillian Trasher, a missionary to Egypt (1910) who broke her engagement to answer God's call, served Egyptian children for fifty years without furlough. When she died in 1961, she was greatly honored by the Egyptian government for her social service, taking care of fourteen hundred children and widows at the orphanage in Assiout, Egypt. In fifty years, she ministered to more than twenty thousand children and widows.

CHALLENGES AND CONCLUSION

God does not call people based on gender, race, abilities, education, or economic status but calls both men and women to fulfill his work. Pentecostals assert that God endows power to those of his people who act in faith and obedience, nothing else. David Roebuck remarks about the early stage of Pentecostal women ministers:

> In almost every case discussed, a female minister significantly influenced these women's understanding of their call to ministry. Without denigrating the role of the Holy Spirit or of the significant males in their lives, the presence of a powerful female role model was remarkable.[43]

If we acknowledge that the call and empowerment of God applies to males as well as females, a woman's role in various ministries such as teaching, preaching, leadership, mission, and administration should be

41. Cavaness, "God Calling," 59.
42. Cavaness, "God Calling," 58.
43. Roebuck, "Go and Tell My Brother," 18.

recognized and even encouraged without limitation. However, in churches, almost all leadership positions are taken by men, who have powerful voices for decision-making. It is interesting that in most congregations, there are more female than male members. This gender imbalance in leadership is also common in institutions and mission organizations. This is particularly true among Asian churches because of their male-dominated culture. Thus, Christian women in Asia have more challenges to overcome.

Women should be given an opportunity for higher education through which they can develop their academic skills. According to Ruth Peever, a TESOL professor at Asia Pacific Theological Seminary and a former missionary in China for fifteen years, who delivered a lecture on the advantages of higher education among young people in Korea in August 2001, her experience in China was that her doctoral degree suddenly opened many doors, especially to places that were exclusive and had a high profile, for ministry. The president of a university in China honored her for her high academic degree. Asian women should be encouraged to strive for higher education and educational challenges for better involvement in ministry.

Women's ordination is not permitted in many denominations in Asia. A simple answer from a denominational leader in Korea was, "You'd better get married." I do not have a strong desire to be ordained; however, ordination may open doors for ministry that would not be available without the ordained position.

Pentecostal denominations have stood out in this socio-ecclesial culture of Asia. Although not uniform, most Pentecostal denominations of Asia have ordained women for ministry. For instance, the General Councils of the Assemblies of God in countries like the Philippines, Malaysia, and Singapore have an impressive proportion of women ministers. In Korea, the number is also rapidly rising. Their achievements are especially noticeable in the mission. However, when we look at their leadership role, we see that it is still male-dominant.

Christ liberated all humanity, including women, on the cross. Pentecostals should endeavor to liberate women in every area of ministry, not just in a few selected areas like Christian education. Historically, the Pentecostal movement liberated social outcasts, like Native Americans, women, and laity. Since we know that God called and empowered both women and men, they must have the same opportunities to fulfill their calling.[44]

44. For example, Cheryl Bridges Johns, "Pentecostals and the Praxis of Liberation," 11, notes that "the active presence of the Holy Spirit . . . calls for a radical balance in the ministry of males and females, blacks and whites, rich and poor."

Women also have to try to improve themselves. Thus, women must encourage themselves and one another. The bottom line is that everyone, man or woman, should have a chance to fulfill their God-given calling.

7

Changing Image

Women in Asian Pentecostalism

WHILE CONTEMPLATING THE TOPIC, Paul's words to the Corinthian church came to mind: "For man did not come from woman, but woman from man; neither was man created for woman, but woman for man" (1 Cor 10:8–9). These words require an exegetical analysis to provide adequate guidance today. The image of women has been changing rapidly in most societies, except in some closed Muslim and communist countries. Surprisingly, women can now fill prominent positions in many professions. Even less than a decade ago, most Asian countries were primarily male-dominated, and to a certain degree, this continues. However, what we see today could never have been envisioned in previous decades. The image of the fragile woman is gradually vanishing. Women are portrayed as essential figures in the media and appear in all forms of advertising today. Attracting the attention of women and children is a crucial part of contemporary business.

This chapter aims to discuss the image of women from biblical and contemporary cultural perspectives and to explore the changing role of women in society, especially in Asia. An underlying question I will explore is: To what degree can we expect the place of women to be transformed and expanded in the church today? This question brings unique challenges and opportunities for the church, especially in Asia.

CHANGES IN THE IMAGE OF WOMEN

Change marks our society, which is seen at the social, political, and economic levels. Likewise, the image of women today differs from the prevalent image in former times, clearly showing that cultural perceptions are not static but dynamic.

The Image of Women in the Biblical World

During the Second Temple period, Jewish women were separated from men in the synagogues.[1] This symbolized male authority over and superiority over women. For the same reason, women were not allowed to study the Torah, and it was assumed that women were not expected to learn or were thought incapable of learning. Even if some women were literate, they could not read aloud during gatherings. Furthermore, women were not permitted to pray in public places or at home (e.g., at mealtimes). Their role was confined solely to the house, caring for the family and the children. Precisely because such discrimination against women was widespread in the first-century Jewish diaspora, it may have been inherited by the early church.[2]

Granted that Hellenistic culture in the first century may have been less restrictive than Jewish culture, there was also clearly discrimination against women in Hellenistic perceptions and practices. This ancient saying is attributed to Aristotle: "Woman is an embarrassment to man, a beast in his quarters, a continual worry, a never-ending trouble, a daily annoyance, the destruction of the household, a hindrance to solitude, the undoing of a virtuous man, an oppressive burden, an insatiable bee, a man's property, and possession."[3] The Palestinian Josephus, a well-known historian of Jewish affairs, the son of Matthias, and a priest of Jerusalem, said, "The woman, says the Law, is in all things inferior to the man. Let her accordingly be submissive, not for her humiliation, but that they may be directed; for God has given the authority to the man."[4]

1. Josephus, *Antiquities of the Jews in the Words of Flavius Josephus*, 431.

2. Pagels, *Gnostic Gospels*, 140–41.

3. Healy, *Women According to Saint Bonaventure*, 46. See also Tucker, *Woman in the Maze*, 156.

4. Oberg, "Trouble-Quiet Sowers of Unrest."

The New Testament depiction of the early church portrays a male-dominated culture, providing little opportunity for women to take leadership roles in public worship and life. Paul lived amid a cultural milieu that viewed women as intellectually inferior and subordinate to men. He argued that women should be silent in public worship (1 Cor 14:34–35; 1 Tim 2:11–12), and he did not allow women to minister in church: "I do not permit a woman to teach or to have authority over a man" (2:12). Paul also asked Timothy to instruct women "to dress modestly with decency and with propriety, not with braided hair or gold or pearls or expensive clothes, but with good deeds, appropriate for women who profess to worship God" (2:9–10). It was understood that prostitutes wore worldly dress. Therefore, it is plausible that such restrictions discouraged women from participating in church gatherings and activities, while most church members would have been male.[5]

What, then, is Paul's intent? It should be remembered that his epistles are ad hoc literature, as Gordon Fee argues.[6] Most likely, Paul intended not to offer a universal prohibition on women in ministry but to address specific congregational situations (1 Tim 2:11–15; 1 Cor 14:34–35).

Despite the cultural tendency to limit women's role, Paul affirms women's role in ministry (teaching, prophesying, etc.) elsewhere. Reading the New Testament carefully shows that the early church challenged its social and religious cultural norms. Women are found teaching (Acts 18:26) and prophesying (Acts 21:9 and 1 Cor 11:5). Phoebe is called a "deacon" (Rom 16:1–2), while Priscilla was Paul's co-worker (16:3). I will not try to portray Paul as being larger than life, as he must also have been a man of his own culture. However, it is fair to state that Paul was "inclusive" concerning the role of women in the church, to the extent that some women were his partners in the work for God's kingdom. His actions thus did not conform to the prevalent cultural conventions regarding women (16:1–2).[7]

Modern Images of Woman

Modern images of women span the "traditional" to "liberated" spectrum. On the one hand, the traditional understanding of women has been tied to their ability to produce children. Their roles as homemakers and caretakers

5. Josephus, *Antiquities of the Jews in the Words of Flavius Josephus*, 431.
6. Fee and Stuart, *How to Read the Bible Book by Book*, 315.
7. Murphy, *Word According to Eve*, 178.

of the family are a natural outgrowth of this responsibility. This traditionalist view continues to significantly restrict women's social roles in many parts of the world. For example, in traditionalist Korea, most married women have perennially been housekeepers, doing household chores and rearing children. If a woman lived with her parents-in-law, her domestic obligations increased drastically. Despite improvements in many developing countries, traditional male dominance remains entrenched, especially in regions where the patriarchal structure is deeply rooted.[8] My experiences as a missionary and a scholar over the past two decades leads me to believe that women's participation in most international events is far less than their male counterparts. Often, women's voices are reluctantly heard, if heard at all.

Yet, on the other hand, in many parts of the contemporary world, this traditional image of women has changed. Since the Enlightenment, there have been arguments against the traditional subordination of women to men, insisting on "the ontological identity of all human beings (all human beings are equal because all partake universally in human nature)."[9] As a result, women have emerged as leaders in prominent positions. The traditional image of women as only good housekeepers no longer holds, and their capabilities within a social community are now respected. There is always the possibility of change.[10]

THE CONTRIBUTIONS OF WOMEN IN CONTEMPORARY SOCIETIES

Some of these changes have been quite dramatic, resulting in women in positions of authority and power. There have been various examples of women in the highest political places in the West—e.g., Catherine the Great brought Russia out of feudalism; Joan of Arc united the dispirited troops of France, pulling along a frightened crown prince into battle and victory; and Queen Elizabeth I ended the bloodbath of religious persecution, and her long reign allowed for a golden age of new ideas and exploration.[11] Has this been the case in Asia? In the following paragraphs, I highlight two

8. Battersby, *Gender and Genius*, 10.

9. Le Guin, "Bryn Mawr Commencement Address," 5. See also Connor, *Theory and Cultural Value*, 159.

10. Anderson, *Giorgione*, 20.

11. Cunningham, "Your Gifts and Destiny," 45–56.

contemporary women who serve as exemplars of change in the Asian context and discuss other changes related to the role of Asian women in the public sphere.

Corazon Aquino: Former President of the Philippines

People remember Aquino as "the bespectacled woman in her trademark yellow dress."[12] She acknowledged that she never imagined becoming a political figure, although politics was in her family's history. Aquino was born into a wealthy and politically prominent family on January 25, 1933. Her parents, Jose Cojuangco, a three-term congressman, and Demetria Sumulong, a pharmacist and daughter of a senator, were among the most influential names in Central Luzon. She achieved her education in the United States: elementary and high school at Saint Scholastica's College and Notre Dame Convent School in New York, and a bachelor of arts in French and mathematics at Mount Saint Vincent Convent, New York. In 1956, she was planning to take up law at the Far Eastern University when Benigno Servillano Aquino Jr. (1932–83) came into her life.[13]

Not too long after her husband was assassinated in 1983 by government agents—he was, after all, the chief political opponent of then President Ferdinand Marcos—Aquino decided to run for the presidency. After the election (1986), she, as well as Marcos, claimed to have won. When Marcos refused to step down, Aquino planned strikes. With the country on the edge of civil war, Marcos decided to fly to the United States as a refugee, and Aquino assumed the presidency. She became the country's first woman president and served until 1992.[14]

Some of Aquino's achievements are summarized as follows: "The movement led by Cory against the dictatorial rule resulted in the 'People Power Revolution' that overthrew the Marcos government in February 1986. Once in power, Cory ordered all political prisoners to be freed and built the machinery for democracy."[15] Yet, while Aquino promised changes and improvements, most did not materialize during her term in office. Economic hardships and incompetent leadership plagued the nation. The continual political struggles and natural calamities that ensued endangered the

12. This is what Filipinos express about Aquino's image as a woman.

13. Editors of Encyclopedia Britannica, "Corazon Aquino."

14. "Aquino, Corazon."

15. "Aquino, Corazon."

gains made by her administration. Her presidency survived seven military revolts, typhoons, drought, an energy crisis, a significant earthquake, and a volcanic eruption. However, Aquino gained the world's attention: "She received several international awards, including Time Magazine's Woman of the Year, the Eleanor Roosevelt Human Rights Award, the United Nations Silver Medal, and the Canadian International Prize for Freedom. She was cited for setting the example of a nonviolent democracy movement later tested in Burma, South Africa, Poland, and Chile."[16]

Myoeng Sook Han: Prime Minister of South Korea

Han, born on March 24, 1944, was the prime minister of South Korea. She completed her BA in French literature and MA in women's studies at Ewha Women's University in Seoul. Han was the first Minister of Gender Equality (2001–3) and also served as the Minister of Environment (2003–4). In March 2006, following the resignation of Prime Minister Lee Hae Chan, President Roh Moo Hyun nominated Han to become the first female prime minister of South Korea. Han was only the second woman nominated for the prime minister's position. In the following month, she was officially sworn in. Her focus was on building international relationships, and she traveled to the United Arab Emirates, Kazakhstan, and Uzbekistan.[17]

Korea is a conservative society that hardly acknowledges women in leadership roles. Hence, her appointment was considered rather radical in the Korean context, and she was under close and constant scrutiny by the public. Tong Kim, the former senior interpreter at the US State Department and visiting scholar at Johns Hopkins School of Advanced International Studies, suggested that Han's work influenced the prospects of the Grand National Party woman leader, Park Geun-hye, in Park's candidacy for the 2007 presidential election. On the one hand, some observers contended that the idea of a woman president was a bit too early for Korea. On the other hand, Korea has a history of having had three queens ruling the Silla kingdom. For this reason, Han's performance had profound implications for the future of women's leadership in Korea.[18]

16. "Aquino, Corazon."
17. BBC News, "First Woman PM."
18. BBC News, "First Woman PM."

Others in the Public Square

When I was growing up, I hardly saw any married women working in prominent public positions, except teaching in schools. Most companies hired single women, who would lose their jobs once married. But in recent years, spaces have often been created for Asian women, both single and married, to participate actively in public places. One example is Indra Nooyi. Born, raised, and educated in Chennai, India, Nooyi became CEO of PepsiCo (2006–2018). She studied management at Yale and was the first desi (a native Indian) to head a U.S. company of that size.[19]

PepsiCo was one of the two largest US companies run by a woman. Besides women like Aquino and Han, others are also increasingly found in political leadership positions. The First Asia-Pacific Congress of Women in Politics was held in Manila, Philippines, from June 21–23, 1994, under the theme "Why Women, What Politics?" The conference was attended by 250 Asian politicians from 23 countries, who discussed their plans to transform politics in Asia.[20] Senator Leticia Shahani, the convener of the Third World Conference on Women held in Nairobi, Kenya, in 1985, was the keynote speaker on the first day of the conference. She emphasized that more women needed to get involved in the electoral process. This would be one way for women to gain access to primary decision-making positions where women could help shape a better and more sustainable world. At the concluding ceremony, President Fidel V. Ramos of the Philippines was a guest of honor who shared his administration's promise to include more qualified women in leadership positions. "He challenged the Philippine delegation in the Congress to come up with names of women whom he could include on his short list of nominees to key positions in his administration."[21] Discussions were focused on two major concerns: (1) to declare the rightful place of women in the public square, and (2) to redefine the notion and exercise of politics and power.

Progressive Trends on the Role of Asian Pentecostal Women

Gender roles are traditionally one of the more challenging areas. However, it has changed in that women are given opportunities to be involved in

19. Seyfferth, "First Asia-Pacific Congress of Women in Politics."
20. Seyfferth, "First Asia-Pacific Congress of Women in Politics."
21. Seyfferth, "First Asia-Pacific Congress of Women in Politics."

leadership, ministry, and other activities. Within Pentecostal churches, gender roles and expectations can be complex and vary greatly based on regional, denominational, and cultural circumstances. Here are some important details regarding gender roles and expectations in Pentecostal congregations.

Gender Role

Traditionally, men have leadership roles and have dominated leadership positions in many Pentecostal churches. While certain Pentecostal denominations are more progressive than others, many continue to enforce gender norms that prevent women from assuming leadership positions. However, some Pentecostal churches and denominations encourage women to hold leadership positions. Women work as church leaders, evangelists, and pastors, and their efforts are being more acknowledged. Many Pentecostal churches have welcomed women into leadership positions in various ministry areas, including community outreach, conference speaking, and worship leading. This indicates a more significant movement in some Pentecostal groups toward gender inclusion.[22]

Women also preach and teach in Pentecostal groups, though usually with specific restrictions. Women may be permitted to run women's organizations or teach Sunday school, but they may not be able to lead sizable crowds or deliver sermons from the pulpit. The Pentecostal movement, particularly within independent churches and some denominations, supports women's ordination and active participation as pastors and preachers. This practice highlights the movement's focus on the Holy Spirit's empowerment of all believers, regardless of gender, for ministry and leadership roles.

Spiritual Empowerment

Pentecostal-Charismatic female empowerment in the United States can be traced back to the emergence of women's suffrage during the early 1900s, a time of great social upheaval brought on by industrialization, urbanization, and World War I that led to large-scale migrations of people from their former communities into new cities, economics, and places of employment.

22. Artman, "Producing Change," 165–85.

As Nanlai Cao notes in "Gender, Modernity, and Pentecostal Christianity in China" in *Global Pentecostalism in the 21st Century*, "Women search for Charismatic power by embracing asceticism, supernaturalism, and emotional revivalism, which underlay the development of early Chinese Pentecostalism amid social and political chaos." This is also evident in Wenzhou, China, as Cao notes, because "she is boss in the domestic sphere while the man is boss in the business sphere," and women in Asia place importance on their homes. Thus, women are naturally suited for home groups. Male pastors "need to recruit subjects who will be faithful to them [and] only those who faithfully heed the call of an event in this way are . . . subjects who work for change," which makes it possible for women to lead in home changes.[23]

Female Pentecostals were actively founding churches and evangelistic centers as well as providing healing services to people as early as the 1950s in Singapore and Malaysia. "Women were instrumental in organizing national assemblies in several Asian AG organizations, or they became the first Pentecostal missionaries."[24] "Remarkable in a male-dominated society like Korea is the number of women who have become pastors of a church and most of the house group leaders are women," said Yonggi Cho of Yoido Full Gospel Church, one of the biggest megachurches in the world. It notes, "equality has liberated those who have traditionally been marginalized in the church; in early Pentecostal ministry and mission settings, women were just as active as men."[25]

Spiritual empowerment is a very significant aspect for women when playing leadership roles. Pentecostal theology strongly emphasizes the gifts of the Holy Spirit available to all Christians, regardless of gender.

OPPORTUNITIES: WHAT SIGNIFICANT IMPACTS COULD ASIAN PENTECOSTAL WOMEN MAKE?

Asian Pentecostal women have contributed significantly to society in various capacities, most notably through their work in social services, education, activism, and religious institutions. Here is a closer look at their influence.

23. Cao, "Gender, Modernity, and Pentecostal Christianity in China," 83.

24. Cheong, "Attenuation of Female Empowerment Among Three Pentecostal Charismatic Chinese Churches," 477–99.

25. Ma, "Women at Yoido Full Gospel Church," 267–84.

Firstly, spiritual influence: Women have been foundational to the growth and spiritual dynamism of Pentecostal movements, initially celebrated for their fervor and granted leadership roles that became constrained by organizational structures over time. Despite facing institutional barriers, women in Pentecostal movements have continued to play pivotal roles, from early trailblazers like Lucy Farrow and Aimee Semple McPherson to contemporary leaders such as Sarah Omakwu and Esther Ibanga, showcasing leadership diversity and social outreach.[26] A few Korean women who have had a significant spiritual effect and leadership impact in Asia are Jashil Choi on the prayer mountain, Seenok Ahn on Bible-based education, and Youjung Kim on a strong and sincere prayer life. Actress Kong Duen Yee, also called Mui Yee, was instrumental in her Pentecostal revival gatherings in Malaysia. Pandita Ramabai has profoundly influenced women's and children's revival movements in India.[27] Women frequently act as church planters, evangelists, and pastors, defying gender stereotypes and advancing the spiritual development of their communities.

Secondly, gender equality: Scholars have traditionally classified the feminist movement into three waves, with the current fourth wave occasionally included. The first wave of feminism (1848–1920) achieved essential advancements in women's suffrage, education, property rights, and the abolition of slavery in the late nineteenth and early twentieth centuries. Amid the whirlwind of ideas surrounding first-wave feminism, women started to theologize about their calling and experiences. These early egalitarian theologians included social revolutionaries in their ranks.[28] Asian Pentecostal women frequently advocate for gender equality inside and outside their communities. They challenge traditional gender stereotypes in favor of women's empowerment and acknowledgment in various disciplines.

Thirdly, Human Rights: The UN declared in 2011 a very significant area of human rights that is incompatible with the allowable limitation to use such legislation to censor or withhold material of substantial public interest that does not endanger national security. It will never be consistent with the allowable limitation to prosecute researchers, journalists, environmental activists, human rights advocates, or anybody else for distributing such knowledge. All public individuals, including presidents of state and government, who wield the most significant political authority, are also

26. Clifton, "Sexism and the Demonic in Church Life and Mission," 62–63.

27. Ma, "Influence of Pentecostal Spirituality to Asian Christianity," 112–13.

28. Evans, "What Makes a (Third) Wave?," 409–28.

entitled to criticism and political opposition. It should not be illegal to criticize institutions like the army or the government; additionally, the UN Human Rights Council (2016) reiterated that political or state interest does not equate to public order or national security.[29]

The constitutions and legal frameworks of several Southeast Asian nations, such as Thailand, the Philippines, and Indonesia, have long recognized human rights related to the environment. However, how the norm is maintained has been significantly impacted by these countries' extractive sectors. The many human rights laws in these nations emphasize how crucial it is to safeguard the procedural aspects of the right to a healthy environment, such as judicial access, to guarantee that the substantive right is upheld in real life.[30]

A wage earner who works in a (private) household under any technique and for any time for compensation is known as a domestic worker. They may work for one or more employers but are not paid for their labor. Most domestic workers are adult women who freely relocate across nations for employment in the domestic services industry. Because low-skilled labor is often associated with gender stereotypes, women may be mainly lured to domestic work abroad. In developing nations, where labor migration has increasingly become a structural survival strategy for migrants and their families, they are frequently recruited from the most vulnerable groups.[31]

Justice has not been served to victims of extrajudicial killings in Indonesia, Cambodia, or the Philippines who were expressing their freedom of speech. Even worse, they have passed and put into effect ambiguous rules that may be used to arrest anyone for trying to express disapproval, criticism, or even just observations. These new, legalized methods of repression violate international human rights norms and legal frameworks.[32]

Some Asian Pentecostal and non-Pentecostal women work on more general human rights concerns, like social justice advocacy, the fight against human trafficking, and the defense of the rights of the underprivileged. Their work frequently touches on international social change movements.

29. Reynolds, "Human Rights in the Age of Southeast Asian Extractivism."

30. Reynolds, "Human Rights in the Age of Southeast Asian Extractivism."

31. Alcoran-Benavidez and Benavidez, "Resilience and Spirit-Empowered Communities," 154–64.

32. Reynolds, "Human Rights in the Age of Southeast Asian Extractivism."

CONCLUDING REMARKS

I intend not to downgrade men or belittle their abilities in this study. Instead, I seek to encourage and empower women to exercise their God-given talents and gifts for God's kingdom. I have never placed myself among feminists nor sought to fight for or insist on women's rights. It is time for Asian Pentecostal churches to contribute to the paradigm shift in our society by living out its inherent theological valuation of women. I hope our discussion will encourage women to envision the possibilities regarding their contributions to God's kingdom and also prompt men to empower women to express their God-given gifts and talents.

I close by again mentioning the courageous life of Huldah Buntain, the wife of a Pentecostal missionary, as even after her husband's death, she continued the mission work in India. In an endorsement of a book on their ministry, Ken Dobson writes: "I wondered what life would be like for Huldah now in India, so far from family, and alone. Surely, if anyone deserved to retire from ministry, it is Auntie Huldah."[33] However, authentic leaders do not just retire, which applies to women and men.

33. Donaldson and Dobson, *Huldah Buntain*, 18.

8

The Spirit-Empowered Ministry of Pentecostal Women

NUMEROUS UNEXPECTED LEADERSHIP ACCOMPLISHMENTS by women have long been highlighted in the Pentecostal/Charismatic tradition. While some Pentecostal and Charismatic women have been able to overcome obstacles, many more have countenanced covert and overt efforts to limit their participation. Additionally, the historical record has been substantially shaped and used as a reference point by male perspectives, even when it recognizes the achievements of women. The opportunities and restrictions Pentecostal and Charismatic women have encountered in their dedication to religious service have elicited diverse reactions.[1]

The experiences of Pentecostal women show, both in the West and non-West, that they have faced more challenges than their male counterparts. Often, their social identity, autonomy, agency, and even theological orientation handicapped them.[2]

The belief that the Holy Spirit, through the impartation of charismata or "spiritual gifts" (see 1 Cor 12 and 14; and Acts 2), or the Spirit's empowerment, enables women to do things they would generally be unable to do due to traditional social restrictions, limitations, and role assignments is perhaps the theme that stands out more than any other. This breaking down of walls has given Pentecostal women in the past and present a sense of seemingly endless ministry possibilities and has served as many women's

1. Alminana, "Introduction," 1.

2. Alminana, "Introduction," 1.

beginning points. Neither politics nor even economics is the primary driver of this empowerment.[3]

This chapter showcases the characteristics of Pentecostal women who courageously accepted their leadership positions in the church and actively served God's kingdom. The cases also illustrate their extraordinary sensitivity to human needs and the Spirit's leadership, thus participating in various ministries that supported the underprivileged, outcasts, and abandoned. Their impact and contributions exceeded all expectations. The case studies will also illustrate their challenges, particularly from the established ecclesiastical orientations and theological perspectives. By overcoming these and other challenges, they exemplify the transformative power of the Holy Spirit.

PANDITA RAMABAI OF INDIA

As an Indian woman who was converted to Christianity, Pandita Ramabai (1858–1922) was known as a "reformer, Bible translator, and social activist and notably, revival movement in her mission." Ramabai rejected the Hindu social norms of "propriety" and the marriage system, leaving the Brahmin caste and turning to God. Less than two years after her marriage, she and her daughter experienced widowhood. During her three years in England, where she studied at Cheltenham Ladies College, she started attending church. She underwent water baptism in the Church of England in 1883. Later, in America, she earned a degree in education.[4]

Pandita Ramabai was well known for her divisive opinions on religion and social problems. Her interpretation of the Christian concept of the Trinity was one of her contentious viewpoints. Ramabai thought that the patriarchal and hierarchical Western society was reflected in the traditional Christian doctrine of the Trinity, which asserts that there is one God in three persons: the Father, the Son, and the Holy Spirit. She claimed that this theory was employed to defend the subordination of women and other socially excluded groups. Instead, Ramabai proposed a new understanding of the Trinity called the "Trinity of Love." According to this view, the three people of the Trinity were Love, Wisdom, and Power. Ramabai argued that this view emphasized the importance of love, equality, and mutual respect

3. Alminana, "Introduction," 1.

4. Anderson, *Spreading Fires*, 77.

in relationships and challenged the patriarchal power structures of society.[5] Within Christian communities, Ramabai's opinions on the Trinity were disputed and were called heretical and even unorthodox by some. Many people, however, also connected with her interpretation of the Trinity because they saw it as a question of social and gender norms.[6]

Engaging in Mission Among the Neglected

After finishing her studies, she returned to India in 1889 and founded a ministry for widows close to Bombay (now Mumbai), which was later relocated to Pune. She established a mission in 1895 on a farm she had bought in Kedgaon, a town adjacent to Pune. By this point, she had transformed her work from a "religiously neutral" community into an overtly "evangelical Christian organization."[7] Her support among Hindu parents disappeared due to this open Christian identity, and her committee later resigned. This mission was given the name "Mukti," meaning "salvation," by Ramabai and her team. Its main objective was to provide marginalized young women and girls a haven. Many of them were widows because of child marriage. Because there was a food shortage, other people were saved from famine. In 1896, there were forty-eight girls and young women, but three hundred girls were rescued from starvation in Madhya Pradesh. Nearly two thousand people had been taken care of by 1900.[8]

Before its revival in 1905, this mission gained notoriety abroad. Ramabai was sure Hindu women could enjoy ultimate freedom by turning to Christ. Her mission also offered training in techniques for earning money. Ramabai's solid mission vision progressed, but by 1907, the Mission had expanded to include a rescue mission, a hospital, an oil press, a blacksmith forge, a printing press, a complete school that provided college entrance training, a school for the blind, and training departments in teaching, nursing, weaving, tailoring, bread and butter making, tinning, laundering, masonry, carpentry, and farming.[9]

5. Jamir, *Theological Quest of an Indian Woman*, 1–2.
6. Jamir, *Theological Quest of an Indian Woman*, 1–2.
7. Anderson, *Spreading Fires*, 77.
8. Mair, *Bungalows in Heaven*, 87–88.
9. Shivananda, *Mukti Prayer-Bell*, 21–22.

Refreshing Experience of the Holy Spirit

Ramabai was quite familiar with the work of the Holy Spirit and had a great belief in it. She once confessed, "I considered it a wonderful blessing to realize the intimate presence of the Holy Spirit in me and to be guided and taught by Him." Her desire to be "filled with the Spirit" to "enter into a fresh experience of God's ability to save, bless, and use" later became very strong. She communicated with Manoramabai and Minnie Abrams to study the requirements of a revival in 1904 after learning of the Welsh Revival and the Australian Revival led by R. A. Torrey. This exchange persuaded her that "pouring out your life and prayer" were essential for revival. Thus, Ramabai established a "special early morning daily prayer meeting, when 70 ladies would meet and pray" in January 1905. She pledged her support for "a special outpouring of the Holy Spirit on all Christians of every region" and "for the true conversion of all the Indian Christians, including us." The attendance at this daily prayer group rapidly increased to five hundred people. Eventually, the Holy Spirit outpoured upon the people who prayed and longed for revival. The revival lasted for an additional year and a half, and its impact was widespread: eleven hundred baptisms at the school, sins confessed and repented of, protracted prayer services, and the observation of seven hundred of these young women dispersing in groups into the neighborhood to preach the gospel. Two hundred young ladies who wanted to create "Praying Bands" and "be schooled in the preaching of their religion" joined her, which she also started. As far as Ramabai was aware, there had never been a renaissance life before 1905.[10]

After the Mukti revival, Mukti teams were invited to tour various locales up until mid-1906, and when they did, revivals began. Fifty preachers and eleven congregations attended the conference held by the Mukti team, headed by Minnie Abrams, in Aurangabad. Abrams served as the conference's keynote speaker. It happened again during that convention: a revelation. The Bangalore revival began in a girls' orphanage and expanded to the neighborhood churches. The beginning of those revivals was greatly aided by the prayer teams of young women from Ramabai's Mukti complex. The renewal impacted the Christian and Missionary Alliance, London Missionary Society, Young Men's and Women's Christian Associations, and Anglicans, Baptists, Lutherans, Methodists, and Presbyterians.[11]

10. Anderson, *Spreading Fires*, 78–79.

11. Anderson, *Spreading Fires*, 81–83.

Missionaries and their Chilean friends started praying to the Lord for a comparable outpouring of the Holy Spirit after hearing about the Mukti Revival in Valparaiso, Chile, in 1907. When believers began confessing their sins during a prayer gathering, their prayers were heard. Then there were manifestations, such as "tongues, visions, trances, laughter, and weeping. The [manifestations] bore the product of transformed lives. From there, the movement expanded to other congregations in Chile (1909 Chile Revival)."[12]

KATHRYN KUHLMAN OF THE UNITED STATES OF AMERICA

Kuhlman held a service in Denver, Colorado, in 1933 to open the Kuhlman Revival Tabernacle (later renamed the Denver Revival Tabernacle). Some healings occurred. A woman claimed, "Last night, while you were preaching, I was healed." Kuhlman asked, "Where were you?" "Just sitting here in the audience . . . I had a tumor. My doctor diagnosed it. While you were preaching, something happened in my body. I was so sure I was healed that I returned to my doctor this morning and had it verified. The tumor is no longer there."[13]

Television impacted the more enormous, profound change in American Christianity that Kuhlman used to illustrate the talk show format. Television Christianity altered how the Christian message was communicated and received beyond merely providing a new platform for evangelism and revival. Her program, *I Believe in Miracles*, had a significant role in the evolution of charismatic Christianity and American Christianity in general, which was brought about by the medium of television. *I Believe in Miracles* was a collection of first-person accounts from followers of charismatic Christianity. Most of the programs featured regular individuals sharing unusual tales that included elements of charismatic Christianity as it evolved during the Charismatic Renewal Movement from the middle of the 1960s to the present. People interested in charismatic Christianity could listen to individuals who appeared to be very average speak about astonishingly outstanding manifestations of the Spirit. Kuhlman's program was available to watch if someone wanted to learn more about divine healing. Due to

12. Anderson, *Spreading Fires*, 80–88.

13. Merrill, *50 Pentecostal and Charismatic Leaders Every Christian Should Know*, 92–93.

Kuhlman's extensive distribution, it was a simple, accessible format and offered a strong option for the viewer. "It was a non-threatening format, readily available . . . . If you didn't like it, you could switch it off, and no one ever need know you 'experimented' with charismatic Christianity."[14] A fascinating episode occurred during the Kuhlman TV show:

> Never had a religious leader hosted a television talk show such as *I Believe in Miracles*. Between 1965 and 1975, during the height of the Charismatic Renewal Movement, healing evangelist and renewal superstar Kathryn Kuhlman hosted a syndicated television show that broke new ground and transformed the practice of Christianity in America. On September 12, 1973, Kathryn Kuhlman welcomed Arlene Strackbein to *I Believe in Miracles* with these words: "My guest today has never seen one of our telecasts. That seems almost impossible when you consider the millions who have." Kuhlman had a propensity for hyperbole, but by 1973 it was safe to say that millions had indeed been exposed to her syndicated television show. During its ten-year run, Kuhlman recorded over 500 episodes of *I Believe in Miracles* broadcast throughout the United States and Canada.[15] *I Believe in Miracles* worked in concert with Kuhlman's best-selling books, popular radio shows, and sold-out Miracle Services to provide the viewing public access to Charismatic Christianity on a scale not seen before. As Kuhlman noted in a conversation with her guest Edna Wilder, "You had never read *I Believe in Miracles*, never seen a telecast, never heard a radio program?" Wilder said no. Kuhlman then exclaimed, "Where in the world have ya been?"[16]

Broadcasting Christianity provided more than a new field for revival and evangelism; it altered how the Christian message was presented and received. *I Believe in Miracles* was a talk show in 1965, a new and groundbreaking arrangement.[17] Kuhlman believed the greatest miracles transpired in worship as the Holy Spirit sovereignly moved through the auditorium. The "circus sideshow" and tent theatrics were unnecessary. As she wrote in *I Believe in Miracles*,[18]

14. Artman, "Producing Change," 165.
15. Artman, "Producing Change," 164.
16. Artman, "Producing Change," 164.
17. Harrell, *All Things Are Possible*, 99–100.
18. King, "Secret to Kathryn Kuhlman's Powerful Healing Ministry," 1.

> No healing virtue in a card or a personality; no necessity for wild exhortations "to have faith." That was the beginning of this healing ministry that God has given me; strange to some because hundreds have been healed just sitting quietly in the audience, without any demonstration whatsoever, and even without admonition. This is because the presence of the Holy Spirit has been so abundant that by His presence alone, sick bodies are healed, even as people wait outside the building for the doors to open.[19]

As she received fresh insight, she adjusted her meetings to accommodate the Holy Spirit's movement better. Kuhlman noted,

> When the power of the Spirit is there, miracles happen. Gradually, I began to understand the power, how it operates. I discovered that certain things brought the presence of the Holy Spirit. Praise, for instance. Just praising God—not asking for anything but just praising Him—always brings power. It's pleasing to the LORD. . . . You do not manipulate the Holy Spirit. The Holy Spirit is a person. He is not an "it." He is God. He is to be reverenced, to be worshiped. He is not to be presumed upon by anyone.[20]

The following Sunday morning, as she preached about the power of the Holy Spirit, a Methodist man with an agonizing manufacturing accident that left him blind and drawing workman's compensation abruptly had tears flowing from his eyes. He could not stop the watering. On the ride home, he blinked, shouting, "I can see! Everything!"[21]

Kuhlman was at the epicenter of a charismatic ministry that was well known worldwide at the time of her death in 1976. Throughout her fifty-five years of preaching, Kuhlman preached to hundreds of thousands of people in front of packed houses. She delivered sermons at monthly services in the seven-thousand-seat Los Angeles Shrine Auditorium to a packed house for the final ten years of her life. Crowds frequently spent hours or even days camping outside the doors before services. She also wrote numerous best-selling books, including *I Believe in Miracles*, a compendium of healing testimonies that have sold over a million copies. Due in part to the efforts of male leaders like Oral Roberts and Benny Hinn, who attempted to claim Kuhlman's posthumous authority as their own, Kuhlman is mostly forgotten in the history of American Christianity despite her outstanding career

19. King, "Secret to Kathryn Kuhlman's Powerful Healing Ministry," 2.

20. King, "Secret to Kathryn Kuhlman's Powerful Healing Ministry," 1.

21. Merrill, *50 Pentecostal and Charismatic Leaders Every Christian Should Know*, 93.

and exceptional popularity. She has been reduced to a cipher, stripped of her personality and narrative, and repurposed by others for their ends.[22]

SPIRIT-EMPOWERED WOMEN MINISTRIES IN AUSTRALIA

Since 1908, the history of Australian Pentecostalism has focused on women's empowerment and has been replete with examples of this similar "outback spirit."[23] Most people have consistently resisted social marginalization by early Pentecostal congregations founded and led by powerful women. Post–World War II women showed incredible strength and endurance. In their missionary endeavors, they overcame gender inequality and ingrained racism while resisting the pressure to submit to the patriarchal culture. Many women persisted in their missional callings. Ironically, they also had to fight the menace of hyper-feminism in the second wave of the feminist movement. They successfully managed to differentiate the empowerment of women from militant feminism.

Surprisingly, the historical background of women's leadership in the Pentecostal movement revealed that women's leadership was well-received and recognized. Joy Langford discussed this well in her article "Feminism and Leadership in Pentecostal Movement" in the *Journal of Feminist Theology*. It notes that the Pioneer movement began in the 1970s due to a church structure led entirely by males. However, as time passed, there was little opposition to women holding leadership and authority roles in the early Pentecostal revivals of the nineteenth and twentieth centuries. Why did it seem as though barriers relating to female leadership were torn down at this time, even though the idea of women in leadership has been a topic of discussion throughout the centuries of church (and social) history? Several vital ideas regarding this matter include: This was a return to biblical Christianity, where women were once more in charge of congregations and missions, following the tenet that power does not permanently reside in those

22. Artman, "Producing Change," 162–63.

23. "The 'outback' is both a literal desert and a mythical place in the Australian identity that represents unchartered opportunities, adventure, and unfamiliar threats. Those who live and exist in the outback thrive in a tough and isolated environment through resourcefulness and hard work. This spirit has generally been incorporated into the psyche of the Australian culture and has become synonymous with such characteristics as defiance, influence, resilience, courage, and ingenuity" (Author Unknown, "Spirit of the Outback," *The Argus*, Sept. 19, 1938, 2). Quoted in Grey, "'Outback Spirit.'"

who wish to serve the church or churches using their position or title. There is no debate over gender because few people argue over who is qualified to serve if authority is to be judged by Holy Spirit–led service.[24]

The Foursquare Gospel Church (ICFG) earlier bragged that 37 percent of its officials were female. Numerous other women worked as missionaries, co-ministers, and pastors. Maria Woodworth-Etter was another outstanding American woman who led the early Pentecostal movement. When she received her Holiness movement preaching license in the 1880s, her meetings rapidly gained popularity, and she started many new churches. Her remarkable ministry was followed by manifestations of God's power, numerous healings, and the conversion of thousands of people to Christ.[25]

Australian women's exceptional resourcefulness has propelled them to international prominence in a rebranded, twenty-first-century "hipster" Pentecostalism.[26] This section will discuss their characteristics and contributions.

Pentecostal women church planters exemplify the Spirit's empowerment to thrive under challenging circumstances and adverse cultural norms. Early twentieth-century Australia placed harsh limitations on women due to economic dependency, family obligations, and denial of civil rights.[27] Pentecostal women, obedient to what they discerned to be God's call, were singularly focused on the lead of the Holy Spirit, disregarding or defying race, gender, and age.[28] Their logic was simple: Who was "man" to stop them if the Spirit had called them?

Methodist lay healing evangelist Sarah Jane Lancaster (1858–1934) established Good News Hall in 1908 and organized Pentecostalism into a denomination, the Apostolic Faith Mission of Australia. Hence, it is not from the Azusa revival meeting. She was known as the unofficial figurehead of early Pentecostalism in Australia.[29] The Apostolic Faith Mission turned to be international—the roots of the Apostolic Faith Mission in South Africa from the Azusa Street Revival. The traditional Pentecostal religious

24. Langford, "Feminism and Leadership in Pentecostal Movement," 28. See also Bartleman, *Another Wave Rolls In*, 32.

25. Langford, "Feminism and Leadership in Pentecostal Movement," 22.

26. Austin and Grey, "'Outback Spirit' of Pentecostal Women Pioneers in Australia," 204–5.

27. Radi, introduction to *200 Australian Women*, 12.

28. Fulkerson, *Changing the Subject*, 253.

29. The AFM was the first formal Pentecostal group in Australia. See Clifton, *Pentecostal Churches in Transition*, 54.

denomination in South Africa is called the Apostolic Faith Mission of South Africa. It is the fifth-largest religious organization in South Africa and the largest Pentecostal congregation, with 1.4 million members, or 7.6 percent of the country's total population.[30]

There were eighteen Pentecostal congregations in Australia by 1925, and eleven had female founders. By 1930, twenty of Australia's thirty-seven Pentecostal congregations were founded and led by women. This cannot be overemphasized because, at the time, women were not even allowed to open bank accounts without their husband's consent.[31]

Lancaster of Good News Hall became a foreboding icon of egalitarianism in Australia. Lancaster and the Hall thrived in the formative years of the Apostolic Faith Mission, which lacked a constitution, ordination, or clerical structure.[32] Despite this, she significantly impacted empowering women in ministry and uniting early Pentecostalism.[33] She earned the title of "Mother" of Australian Pentecostalism.[34]

Together with her husband Lloyd, Edith Averill (1922–2016) served as a conference speaker, author, and church leader over nearly a dozen congregations around Australia.[35] She also acted as matron of Bible colleges in Australia and New Zealand, overseeing the planning of all meals and lodging. She created the first-ever "Women in Ministry" and Students' Wives Fellowships programs. She supported college women, many of whom studied part-time while caring for small children.

Bernice Hall is another early Pentecostal woman pioneer. Hall, a former opera singer, who became a disciple of Kathryn Kuhlman, founded and led the Nollamara Assembly of God in 1962. With around five hundred attendees at the time, it quickly grew to be one of the largest churches in Western Australia.[36]

30. Wikipedia, "Apostolic Faith Mission of South Africa," 296.

31. Austin and Grey, "'Outback Spirit' of Pentecostal Women Pioneers in Australia," 206.

32. Clifton, "Australian Pentecostalism," 305.

33. Austin and Grey, "'Outback Spirit' of Pentecostal Women Pioneers in Australia," 206.

34. Austin and Grey, "'Outback Spirit' of Pentecostal Women Pioneers in Australia," 208.

35. Austin and Grey, "'Outback Spirit' of Pentecostal Women Pioneers in Australia," 212.

36. Austin and Grey, "'Outback Spirit' of Pentecostal Women Pioneers in Australia," 213.

As Pentecostalism rapidly gained recognition worldwide, pioneering Pentecostal women strongly desired to serve as missionaries abroad. Other women who were taken up in the Charismatic Renewal joined the Pentecostals.[37] This occurred for Roman Catholic women after the Second Vatican Council (1962–65) promised improved social fairness and for Protestant women after many denominations eased restrictions on women in church leadership.[38] Some Pentecostal women felt divinely compelled to serve in foreign missions, including Evelyn Westbrook (née Brumpton), who worked in Papua New Guinea for forty years with her husband, Cyril. There were other long-term missionaries in that area, including Glenys Hovey (fifteen years), Lillian Westbrook (twenty years), Elizabeth Evans (fifteen years), Peal Badham (twenty years), and many more.[39] According to research, these female role models helped Papua New Guinean women take on increased leadership roles in their communities.[40]

Besides Pentecostal women's leadership, Judith MacNutt, who led within the Charismatic circle, is noted. She was a clinical psychologist and missionary to Israel. Together with her husband, Francis MacNutt, she established Christian Healing Ministries in Clearwater, Florida, in 1980. She was active and capable of leading the healing prayer and spiritual care.[41] To practice healing prayer and spread its brand of charismatic Christianity, CHM has created schools, workshops, and retreats. Besides her husband's ministry, Judith took over some ministries as president in 2008. She also oversees the ministry and guides the organization with her energizing speaking, charismatic evanescence, and managerial abilities. As a result, CHM has consequences for how women's roles are understood and how they view healing. She is a charismatic speaker whom both women and men respect. She has imprinted on the ministry by fusing Christian therapy and prayer.[42]

Marie Smith (1815–1971) is a famous missionary who battled "postwar racism and gender discrimination to return to her childhood home of

37. Synan, *Holiness-Pentecostal Tradition*, 216.

38. Franklin, introduction to *Opening the Cage*, 1–4.

39. Austin and Grey, "'Outback Spirit' of Pentecostal Women Pioneers in Australia," 214.

40. Dickson-Waiko, "Missing Rib," 103.

41. Althouse, "Women Praying for Women," 370.

42. Althouse, "Women Praying for Women," 370.

Japan and continue the work of her Good News Hall missionary parents."[43] Smith became an eminent preacher nationwide, delineating at one point: "There was a real Pentecostal fervor throughout the meetings. One thrilled at the sight of 800 Christians gathered on a Sunday morning."[44]

It is inconceivable that Australian women like Marie Smith, who overcame racism and gender prejudice by rising to prominence as spiritual leaders, did so. As an illustration, Mary Querro, a well-known Australian Indigenous leader, started Sunday schools in rural areas where many people were transformed, filled with the Holy Spirit, and miraculously healed.[45] More than two hundred individuals, including senior Assemblies of God officials from the US and Japan, attended Smith's burial after she passed away suddenly in Japan.[46] Despite many obstacles, such incredible endurance enabled many women, including Westbrook and Smith, to see their dreams of serving as missionaries abroad come true.

Some Australian Pentecostal women overcame institutional restraints thanks to their "outback spirit" of inventive ingenuity. The secular media regarded Australian Pentecostalism as "prosperous and contemporary" in 2000. Thousands of women "milled about amid the marquees and pots of pink and magenta petunias" during Bobbie Houston's Color Conference, the national director of the Assemblies of God in Australia women's ministry.[47] Contemporary Christian praise music from Australia, which has seen "chart-bending popularity," is largely responsible for this media attention.[48]

Australian Assemblies of God was renamed Australian Christian Churches (ACC) in 2007, and it now includes more than one thousand churches and twenty-eight hundred ordained preachers ministering domestically and abroad. Donna Crouch of Hillsong Church was voted to the ACC National Executive Board in a bold move that year. The international impact of innovative, talented women leaders also influenced

43. Austin and Grey, "'Outback Spirit' of Pentecostal Women Pioneers in Australia," 214.

44. Austin and Grey, "'Outback Spirit' of Pentecostal Women Pioneers in Australia," 214.

45. Austin and Grey, "'Outback Spirit' of Pentecostal Women Pioneers in Australia," 210.

46. Austin and Grey, "'Outback Spirit' of Pentecostal Women Pioneers in Australia," 211.

47. Bagnall, "New Believers," 5–21.

48. Hutchinson and Wolffe, *Short History of Global Evangelicalism*, 261.

national sentiment.[49] This expanding influence results from the Pentecostal and Charismatic movement's phenomenal growth in Australia.

MARGARET BENSON-IDAHOSA OF NIGERIA

Bishop Margaret Benson-Idahosa assumed the complete leadership position after the passing of her husband, Archbishop Benson Idahosa, in 1998. She became the first female Pentecostal bishop in Africa.[50] Archbishop Benson Idahosa, who founded Church of God Mission International, married Margaret Izevbigie on April 6, 1969.[51] As the Presiding Bishop, she oversees thousands of churches with millions of members worldwide. She also serves as the senior pastor of the five-thousand-member Faith Miracle Center Church, with various services each week.[52]

The historical background demonstrates that during a revival movement in the 1930s, the Aladura Pentecostal churches quickly multiplied throughout Yorubaland, becoming a significant aspect of Western Nigerian society. Since Nigeria's independence, the Aladura Church movement has continued to expand; the Christ Apostolic Church is the first Aladura Pentecostal church to exist in Nigeria and one of the biggest churches in the country. It is also represented outside Nigeria in North America, Europe, and other African nations. The breakaway churches established over the past century have strongly emphasized prayer, fasting, and the use of healing waters and oils despite differences in theology, polygamy, and interpersonal dynamics. Because of the CAC's Christological orientation, focus on the Bible, knowledgeable leadership, and educational outreach, the Nigerian government favors it.[53]

Poor and marginalized Nigerians who had little to no influence in the mission churches previously had chances to become active and influential members of their religious communities through the Aladura Pentecostal churches. They also incorporate local symbolism, therapeutic practices, worship traditions, and spiritual roles to create a "contextualized Christianity" that makes the Aladura and other Pentecostal churches attractive

49. Yong, preface to *Philip's Daughters*, vii; see also Pierce, "Woman-tology and the Future Face of Pentecostalism," 381.

50. Fatokun, "Women and Leadership in Nigerian Pentecostal Churches," 1–14.

51. Olofinjana, *20 Pentecostal Pioneers in Nigeria*, 103.

52. Ehijiator, "[Vanguard Awards] Bishop Margaret Idahosa."

53. Anderson, "Aladura Churches," 60–61.

to various Nigerian Christians.[54] In addition to continuing the previous ministries that her husband had begun, Benson-Idahosa also created new ministries. In more than 140 countries across all seven continents, she has preached the gospel of Jesus Christ. Throughout her global church network, she passionately implemented her vision and mission to "reach the underserved." During her husband's reign, the church developed significant humanitarian work. After the passing of her husband in 1998, she elevated it by providing services to the underprivileged and needy in society. She led the church effectively, with over four thousand branch churches nationwide in Africa, Europe, North America, and Asia.[55]

One of the main reasons for her success was the shared vision with her husband for education. They faithfully adhered to Nelson Mandela's maxim "Education is the most potent weapon you can use to change the world."[56] This explains why they exerted tremendous resources in establishing the Benson Idahosa University in Benin City in 1993. The University Institute partners with the University of Benin and Ambrose Ali University, Ekpoma.[57]

Margaret Idahosa, a professional educator, is proud of the Word of Faith Schools she founded. Today, this education system operates more than one hundred kindergarten, primary, and secondary schools across Nigeria and provides scholarships to gifted but low-income students at various universities. Additionally, she offers funds to widows to start small businesses through her foundation so they may support their families without their husbands.[58] Margaret's altruistic act extends to Edo State and all other states and nations where the church has affiliates. As part of its commitment to expanding access to healthcare for all people, the Church of God Mission International (CGMI) founded the Faith Mediplex chain of hospitals in Benin in 1989. In contrast to other church leaders who unwisely advise their people to boycott health care services on the grounds of religion, the initiative portrays CGMI leadership as balanced.[59]

Archbishop Benson Idahosa's purpose was to "blend the hand of prayer with the hand of medicine to treat the full person, mind, and body";

54. Anderson, "Aladura Churches," 60–61.

55. Ehijiator, "[Vanguard Awards] Bishop Margaret Idahosa."

56. Socratic Method, "Nelson Mandela."

57. Ehijiator, "[Vanguard Awards] Bishop Margaret Idahosa."

58. Quisenberry, "Faith Emmanuel Benson Idahosa II."

59. Ehijiator, "[Vanguard Awards] Bishop Margaret Idahosa."

the hospital provides outstanding holistic care. The hospital soon expanded into a multi-specialty teaching hospital complex with numerous training programs and extension facilities in Abuja and Uyo, in Akwa Ibom State. The hospitals offer low-cost or free medical care to churchgoers and non-members, especially the poor.[60]

Bishop Margaret Benson-Idahosa also founded the non-denominational organization known as Christian Women Fellowship International (CWFI). This ministry for female members promotes the education of women to realize their full potential, be good mothers and wives, and serve as tools for end-time evangelism. Membership in this organization includes Americans, Europeans, Africans, and Nigerians. The Restoration Center, a multipurpose edifice with more than ten thousand seats for women, was constructed to fulfill this vision. This Center functions as a conference facility, office space, a center for skill development, and a place to rehabilitate young women in need. Thousands have experienced freedom from bad traditions and spiritual and financial empowerment. A mobile medical clinic that provides free medical services to rural residents has been added to the Restoration Center.[61]

The church members and even outsiders were apprehensive of the church's future at the passing of Bishop Benson Idahosa. But Margaret Idahosa exercised her excellent and visionary leadership to continue and strengthen her husband's incredible legacy. She is a reputable builder, leader, and coordinator with talent and dedication. Indeed, the church has made exponential progress under her pastoral leadership.

CONCLUDING REMARKS

Indian woman Pandita Ramabai's revolutionary ministry influenced hugely neglected widows and children. Ramabai and her colleagues called this expedition "Mukti," which translates to "salvation." Its principal goal was to give marginalized young women and girls a safe place. Due to child marriage, a large number of them were widows. Besides providing for physical needs, she was greatly concerned about their spiritual growth. She sought the presence of the Holy Spirit upon them as her strong desire was for them to experience the power of the Spirit. They began to pray for revival, and

60. Ehijiator, "[Vanguard Awards] Bishop Margaret Idahosa."

61. Quisenberry, "Faith Emmanuel Benson Idahosa II."

those who prayed and yearned for revival received an outpouring of the Holy Spirit. Another year and a half were added to the revival's lifespan.

The evolution of Charismatic Christianity and American Christianity, in general, was facilitated by television, and *I Believe in Miracles* played a significant part in this development. The book *I Believe in Miracles* included a collection of first-person testimonies from Charismatic Christians. During the Charismatic Renewal Movement, which lasted from the middle of the 1960s until the present, people interested in Charismatic Christianity had the chance to hear speakers who seemed very ordinary discuss amazingly extraordinary manifestations of the Spirit. Watching Kuhlman's program to learn more about divine healing was possible.

Pentecostal women in Australia demonstrated fantastic power and endurance after WWII. Despite pressure to conform to the patriarchal culture and pervasive prejudice, they continued with their missionary work. Many female members of the bigger church kept up with their missions. Ironically, though, prominent Pentecostal individuals in Australia are fighting against the threat of hyper-feminism and are still committed to educating women for ministry even as society significantly questions women's empowerment in the messages of second-wave feminism. Due to their outstanding inventiveness, Australian women have now achieved global recognition through a rebranded kind of twenty-first-century modern Pentecostalism.

Margaret Benson-Idahosa's impact is through diverse ministries, including pastoral, holistic, women's ministries, and others that enormously influenced people's lives. Among her most remarkable achievements was the leadership role Bishop Margaret Benson-Idahosa took on following the death of her husband in 1998. She has proven equally competent through her leadership.

Several common themes surfaced by studying the selected Pentecostal and Charismatic women leaders. The first is Spirit-empowerment. They all share the belief in and experience the dynamic work of the Holy Spirit. Healing, miracles, and bold preaching marked their ministries. The second is their unyielding commitment to God's call with resilience in the face of adverse cultural and social forces. The third is their shared passion for suffering and marginalization in society. In addition to evangelism, their ministries included education and social services. The fourth is the outcome of their ministries promoting the rights, equality, and well-being of those they ministered to. The fifth is that women leaders serve as role models for the younger generation, especially girls in deprived social contexts.

They achieved this by battling unjust and unequal systems in the church and society and establishing their identity as God's called and empowered servants.

CONCLUSION

Men and women have new opportunities due to the worldwide Christian movement's seismic upheaval and the swift changes occurring in different cultures and societal structures. Women in the Global South now have the chance to contribute to developing a new worldwide Christianity. Women must take their callings and gifts seriously to impact the world. The gospel and the church must greatly empower women frequently disadvantaged regarding social chances, health, and education. Women pursuing higher education must actively participate in academic circles through various intellectual exercises. Those women, especially in academic circles, will continue their academic engagement.

Pentecostal women have hugely influenced and accomplished in diverse countries through the empowerment of the Holy Spirit. The first woman is Jashil Choi. The unique spirituality of Choi has been an enormous example to the church. Through her pastoral and international ministry, she practically affected millions of believers everywhere she traveled with prayer life and fasting. The prayer mountain was founded by her insisting yet passionate spirit. Yoido Full Gospel Church, where she was the associate pastor, faced financial challenges. Hence, her idea of establishing the prayer mountain was initially unacceptable, but her fervent prayer and not-giving-up attitude eventually convinced the church elders to approve. Fasting and prayer were central to her life and ministry until her passing and influenced local and international Christians to pray with fasting. Her solid spiritual dedication, prayer combined with fasting, and the depth to which it permeated her life astounded many people.

The second woman is Elva Vanderbout. Vanderbout's willingness to sacrifice her life significantly changed many villages. She boldly went into pagan communities where head-hunting was practiced, and she disseminated the priceless and essential message of Christ. Vanderbout had faith that God would keep her safe. The chapter did not fully describe her ministry among the Kankana-ey tribe and other tribes, which appears endless. Her dream of living and serving in the mountains was realized, and she felt content knowing her efforts were not in vain.

The third case is using female members for cell groups. Yonggi Cho's idea to utilize women for the church's cell group structure is a God-given revelation. Some women objected to Cho's ultimate decision to designate female leaders for the cell groups. This demonstrates the extent to which the gender-biased value system was ingrained. Cho only had the requisite persistence and conviction because of the profound awareness of God's vision. He maintained this countercultural framework by carefully training the leaders. The church took pains to uphold these leaders' credentials. They served as the foundation of Cho's church and were his top ministry concern. As a result, the church's spiritual life and membership grew more vibrant and active. The approach has shown itself to be very empowering after decades of use.

The fourth instance is Huldah Buntain's dedication to India. Huldah and her husband, Mark Buntain, gave their lives to people in Calcutta, India. That chapter emphasized the devoted and hardworking missionary work in Calcutta. It is fascinating how their first one-year trip to Calcutta extended to over sixty years. They were there to carry out God's will and purpose for the Calcutta people. The social work of starting different schools, participating in feeding programs, operating a hospital, and many other ministries were new to the Buntains. In addition to receiving food and education, their medical services were of great use to countless youngsters. Adults also benefited from a wide range of excellent social services. These services are crucial in bringing people together.

Examining the chosen Pentecostal and Charismatic female leaders, Pandita Ramabai in India, Kathryn Kuhlman in America, Australian women, and Margaret Benson-Idahosa of Nigeria, revealed some recurring themes. Spirit empowerment comes first. They all believe in and feel the Holy Spirit's active work. Healing, miracles, and fearless preaching characterized their ministries. The second is their steadfast adherence to God's call while being resilient despite unfavorable social and cultural influences. The third is their mutual love for society's disadvantaged and suffering members. Their ministry encompassed social assistance and education in addition to evangelism. The fourth results from their ministries' efforts to advance the equality, rights, and welfare of the people they serve. The fifth is that young people, particularly girls from underprivileged backgrounds, look up to female leaders as role models.

I hope many women are empowered and inspired to use their strengths and abilities to benefit God's kingdom. I have never identified as a feminist, nor have I ever tried to defend or advocate for women's rights. It is time for Asian Pentecostal churches and Pentecostal churches in the world to live out their innate theological value of women and help transform the paradigm in our society. In addition to inspiring women to imagine the potential of their contributions to God's kingdom, I hope this book will encourage men to support women in expressing their divinely endowed abilities.

Bibliography

Aano, Kjetil. "The Church Going Glocal: Mission and Globalisation." https://zoboko.com/text/548oylnr/the-church-going-glocal-mission-and-globalisation/30.

Abeysekera, Fred. *The History of the Assemblies of God of Singapore*. Singapore: Abundant Press, 1992.

Ackerson, Leland. "Korean Confucianism." *Evangelical Review of Theology* 35:2 (2011) 100–110.

Adedipe, Adeyinka. "Margaret Benson-Idahosa: Matriarch of Nigerian Pentecostalism." *Punch*, July 28, 2023. https://punchng.com/margaret-benson-idahosa-matriarch-of-nigerian-pentecostalism/.

African Theology Worldwide. "Global Digital Library on Theology and Ecumenism (GlobeTheoLib)." https://african.theologyworldwide.com/?view=article&id=113&catid=32.

Ahmad, Aminah. *Women in Malaysia*. Manila: ADB, 1998.

———. *Women in the People's Republic of China*. Manila: ADB, 1998.

Ahn, Seenok. *Fasting Prayer*. Audio tapes, Jan. 15, 1988.

Alcoran-Benavidez, Doreen, and Edwardneil Benavidez. "Resilience and Spirit-Empowered Communities: Stories of Overseas Filipino Women Workers in Pentecostal-Charismatic Churches." In *Human Sexuality and the Holy Spirit: Spirit-Empowered Perspectives*, edited by Wonsuk Ma and Kathleen Reid-Martinez, 153–64. Tulsa, OK: Oral Roberts University Press, 2019.

Allen, Leslie, C. "Spirituality of the Psalms." Lecture delivered at the William Menzies Annual Lectureship, Asia Pacific Theological Seminary, Baguio, Philippines, 2001.

Alminana, Margaret. "Introduction: The Purpose and Theoretical Framework of This Book." In *Women in Pentecostal and Charismatic Ministry: Informing a Dialogue on Gender, Church, and Ministry*, edited by Margaret English de Alminana and Lois E. Olena, 1–29. Leiden: Brill, 2017.

Althouse, Peter. "Women Praying for Women: Christian Healing Ministries and the Embodiment of Charismatic Prayer." In *Women in Pentecostal and Charismatic Ministry: Informing a Dialogue on Gender, Church, and Ministry*, edited by Margaret English de Alminana, and Lois E. Olena, 370–83. Leiden: Brill, 2017.

Alvarez, Miguel. "Pentecostals, Society, and Christian Mission in Latin America." In *Pentecostal Mission and Global Christianity*, edited by Wonsuk Ma et al., 301–23. Oxford: Regnum, 2014.

Anderson, Allan. "Aladura Churches." In *Religions of the World: A Comprehensive Encyclopedia of Beliefs and Practices*, edited by J. Gordon Melton and Martin Baumann, 60–71. Santa Barbara, CA: ABC-CLIO, 2010.

———. *Spreading Fires: The Missionary Nature of Early Pentecostalism*. London: SCM, 2007.

Anderson, Jaynie. *Giorgione: The Painter of Poetic Brevity*. Paris and New York: Flammarion, 1997.

"Aquino, Corazon." In *The Columbia Electronic Encyclopedia*, 6th ed. New York: Columbia University Press. https://www.infoplease.com/encyclopedia/history/asia-africa/philippines-bios/aquino-corazon.

Arnold, Clinton. *Ephesians: Exegetical Commentary on the New Testament*. Grand Rapids: Zondervan, 2010.

Artman, Amy Collier. "Producing Change: Kathryn Kuhlman and Modern Media." In *Women in Pentecostal and Charismatic Ministry: Informing a Dialogue on Gender, Church, and Ministry*, edited by Margaret English de Alminana and Lois E. Olena, 165–85. Leiden: Brill, 2017.

Asian Development Bank. *Poverty in Viet Nam*. Manila: ADB, 1997.

Assembly of God Church Kolkata. "Our History." https://agkolkata.org/about/history/.

Augustine, St. "Confessions." In *Devotional Classics*, edited by Richard Foster and James Bryan Smith, 52–85. Peabody, MA: Hendrickson, 1993.

Austin, Denise A., and Jacqueline Grey. "'The Outback Spirit' of Pentecostal Women Pioneers in Australia." In *Women in Pentecostal and Charismatic Ministry: Informing a Dialogue on Gender, Church, and Ministry*, edited by Margaret English de Alminana and Lois E. Olena, 204–26. Leiden: Brill, 2017.

Bagnall, Diana. "The New Believers." *The Bulletin* 118.6219 (2000) 5–21.

Baker, Don. *Dimensions of Asian Spirituality: Korean Spirituality*. Honolulu: University of Hawaii Press, 2008.

Bartleman, Frank. *Another Wave Rolls In: What Really Happened at Azusa Street?* Northridge, CA: Voice, 1970.

Battersby, Christine. *Gender and Genius: Towards a Feminist Aesthetics*. London: Women's Press, 1989.

BBC News. "First Woman PM for South Korea." BBC, July 11, 2002. http://news.bbc.co.uk/2/hi/asia-pacific/2121507.stm.

Benge, Janet, and Geoff Benge. *Lillian Trasher: The Greatest Wonder in Egypt*. Seattle: YWAM, 2004.

Bondi, Roberta C. *To Pray and to Love*. Minneapolis: Fortress, 1991.

Bounds, E. M. *The Complete Works of E. M. Bounds on Prayer*. Grand Rapids: Baker, 1995.

Brock, Charles, and Dottie Brock. *Church Growth Manual*. No 7. Seoul: Church Growth International, 1998.

Buntain Foundation. "About Us." https://buntainfoundation.org/about/.

Buntain, Huldah. "Fifty Years in Calcutta." Christian Broadcasting Network, n.d. https://cbn.com/article/not-selected/huldah-buntain-fifty-years-calcutta.

———. *Treasures in Heaven*. New Kensington, PA: Whitaker, 1982.

Buntain, Mark. *Pathway to the Impossible*. Calcutta: Calcutta Mercy Ministries, 2009.

Cao, Nanlai. "Gender, Modernity, and Pentecostal Christianity in China." In *Global Pentecostalism in the 21st Century*, edited by David Barrett and Steren Notley, 75–98. New York: Oxford University Press, 2012.

Cavaness, Barbara. "God Calling: Women in Assemblies of God Mission." *Pneuma: The Journal of the Society for Pentecostal Studies* 16:1 (1994) 49–62.

Cheong, Weng Kit. "The Attenuation of Female Empowerment Among Three Pentecostal Charismatic Chinese Churches in Malaysia and Singapore in 50 Pentecostal Theology: Practical Application Pentecostal Theology in Politics, Economy and Social Issues." *Pneuma* 41:6 (2019) 477–99.

Cho, Yonggi. "Prayer Can Change the Course of Your Life." *Pentecostal Evangel* 18:4 (1998) 10–23.

Choi, Jashil. *How to Pray for Answer* [in Korean]. Seoul: Seoul Books, 1997.

———. *I Was Mrs. Hallelujah.* Seoul: Seoul Books, 1978.

Church Growth International. *Church Growth Manual.* No 7. Seoul: Church Growth International, 1995.

Clark, Donald. *Culture and Customs of Korea.* Westport, NY: Greenwood, 2000.

Clifton, Shane. "Australian Pentecostalism: Origins, Developments, and Trends." In *Global Renewal Christianity: Spirit Empowered Movements Past, Present, and Future: Asia and Oceana*, edited by Vinson Synan and Amos Yong, 1:294–314. Lake Mary, FL: Charisma House, 2015.

———. *Pentecostal Churches in Transition: Analyzing the Developing Ecclesiology of the Assemblies of God in Australia.* Leiden: Brill Academic, 2009.

———. "Sexism and the Demonic in Church Life and Mission." *Australasian Pentecostal Studies* 11.8 (2009) 51–70.

Clinton, E. Arnold. *Ephesians: Power and Magic.* Grand Rapids: Baker, 1992.

Comskey, Joel. "Rev. Cho's Cell Groups and Dynamics of Church Growth." In *Charis and Charisma: David Yonggi Cho and the Growth of Yoido Full Gospel Church*, edited by Sunghoon Myung and Yonggi Hong, 143–57. Eugene, OR: Wipf & Stock, 2003.

Connor, Steven. *Theory and Cultural Value.* Oxford: Blackwell, 1992.

Cox, James S. "Aladura Churches." In *Religions of the World: A Comprehensive Encyclopedia of Beliefs and Practices*, edited by J. Gordon Melton and Martin Baumann, 60–71. Santa Barbara, CA: ABC-CLIO, 2010.

Cullmann, Oscar. *Christ and Time.* Philadelphia: Westminster, 1964.

Cundall, Arthur E. *Judges and Ruth.* Downers Grove, IL: InterVarsity, 1968.

Cunningham, Loren. "How We Know What We Believe." In *Why Not Women? A Fresh Look at Scripture on Women in Missions, Ministry, and Leadership*, by Loren Cunningham and David Joel Hamilton, with Janice Rogers, 29–44. Seattle: YWAM, 2000.

———. "It's High Time." In *Why Not Women? A Fresh Look at Scripture on Women in Missions, Ministry, and Leadership*, by Loren Cunningham and David Joel Hamilton, with Janice Rogers, 13–27. Seattle: YWAM, 2000.

———. "Your Gifts and Destiny." In *Why Not Women? A Fresh Look at Scripture on Women in Missions, Ministry, and Leadership*, by Loren Cunningham and David Joel Hamilton, with Janice Rogers, 45–56. Seattle: YWAM, 2000.

Dabney, Elizabeth Juanita. *What It Means to Pray Through.* Memphis, TN: Church of God in Christ, 1987.

Department of Planning. "The Statistics of the School in 1999." Daejon, Korea: Daesung Christian School, 1999.

Deuchler, Martina. *The Confucian Transformation of Korea: A Study of Society and Ideology.* Harvard-Yenching Institute Monograph Series. Boston: Harvard University Asia Center, 1995.

Dharamraj, Havilah. "We Reap What We Sow: Engaging Curriculum and Context in Theological Education." *Evangelical Review of Theology* 38:4 (2014) 2–14.

Dickson-Waiko, Anne. "The Missing Rib: Mobilizing Church Women for Change in Papua New Guinea." *Oceania* 74:3 (2003) 90–103.

Donaldson, Hal, and Kenneth M. Dobson. *Huldah Buntain: Woman of Courage.* Springdale, PA: Whitaker House, 1989.

Douglas, Philip D. *Yonggi Cho and the Korean Pentecostal Movement.* Berkeley: University of California Press, 2000.

Editors of Encyclopedia Britannica. "Corazon Aquino." Last updated June 20, 2025. https://www.britannica.com/biography/Corazon-Aquino.

Ehijiator, Kenneth. "[Vanguard Awards] Bishop Margaret Idahosa: Driven by Passion for Humanity 2022." Vanguard News Nigeria, May 20, 2022. https://www.vanguardngr.com/2022/05/vanguard-awards-bishop-margaret-idahosa-driven-by-passion-for-humanity/.

Ehrenreich, Barbara. "For Women." *Time* (Sept. 22, 1995) 10–23.

Eim, Yeolsoo. "The Amazing Ministry of Rev. Dr. Seen Ok Ahn." *Cyberjournal for Pentecostal-Charismatic Research* 1–2 (2024). http://www.pctii.org/cyberj/cyberj6/eim.html.

———. "Pentecostalism and Public School: A Case Study of Rev. Dr. Seen-Ok-Ahn." *The Spirit and Church* 1:1 (1999) 1–22.

Evans, Elizabeth. "What Makes a (Third) Wave? How and Why the Third-Wave Narrative Works for Contemporary Feminists." *International Feminist Journal of Politics* 18:3 (2015) 409–28.

Fatokun, Samson. "Women and Leadership in Nigerian Pentecostal Churches." *Studia Historiae Ecclesiasticae* 32:3 (2006) 1–14.

Fee, Gordon D., and Douglas Stuart. *How to Read the Bible Book by Book.* Grand Rapids: Zondervan, 2002.

Flax, Jane. "Postmodernism and Gender Relations in Feminist Theory." *Signs: Journal of Women in Culture and Society* 12:3 (1987) 23–36.

Florence, Christie. *Called to Egypt.* Wichita Falls, TX: Western Christian Foundation, 1997.

Franklin, Margaret Ann. Introduction to *Opening the Cage: Stories of Church and Gender*, edited by Ruth S. Jones, 1–4. Sydney, Australia: Unwin Hyman, 1987.

Fulkerson, Mary McClintock. *Changing the Subject: Women's Discourses and Feminist Theology.* Eugene, OR: Wipf & Stock, 2000.

Giles, Kevin. *The Trinity and Subordinationism: The Doctrine of God and the Contemporary Gender Debate.* Downers Grove, IL: InterVarsity, 2002.

Globethics. "About Us." https://globethics.net/about-us.

Grey, Jacqueline. "The 'Outback Spirit' of Pentecostal Women Pioneers in Australia." In *2016 SPS Annual Conference Papers: Worship, the Art, and the Spirit*, Oral Roberts University, March 2016.

Hamilton, David. "Women Leaders Too." In *Why Not Women? A Fresh Look at Scripture on Women in Missions, Ministry, and Leadership*, by Loren Cunningham and David Joel Hamilton, with Janice Rogers, 227–31. Seattle: YWAM, 2000.

Harrell, David Edwin, Jr. *All Things Are Possible: The Healing and Charismatic Revivals in Modern America.* Bloomington: Indiana University Press, 1975.

Hartman, Tim. *Kwame Bediako: African Theology for a World Christianity.* Edinburgh: Edinburgh University Press, 2021.

Hayes, Jeanne. "Sowing the Grains of Peace: A Resource Handbook for Building Peace." Paper presented at Northeast Asia Sub-Regional Women's Consultation Ginowan Seminar, Okinawa, Japan, 1992.

Healy, Emma T. *Women According to Saint Bonaventure*. New York: Georgian, 1956.

Hollenweger, Walter J. "Pentecostal Research: Problems and Promises." In *Guide to the Study of the Pentecostal Movement*, edited by Charles E. Jones, vii–ix. Metuchen, NJ: Scarecrow, 1983.

Hurston, John W., and Karen L. Hurston. *Caught in the Web*. Anaheim, CA: Church Growth International, 1981.

Hurston, Karen. *Growing the World's Largest Church*. Springfield, MO: Gospel Publishing House, 1995.

Hutchinson, Mark, and John Wolff. *A Short History of Global Evangelicalism*. Cambridge: Cambridge University Press, 2012.

Hyatt, Susan C. "Spirit-Filled Women." In *the Century of the Holy Spirit: 100 Years of Pentecostal and Charismatic Renewal 1901–2001*, edited by Vinson Synan, 233–62. Nashville: Thomas Nelson, 2001.

Hyman, Paula E. "The Other Half: Women in the Jewish Tradition." *The Jewish Woman: New Interdenominational Theology* 22:2 (1995) 231–40.

Illo, Jeanne Frances. *Women in the Philippines*. Manila: ADB, 1997.

International Theological Institutes. *A History of the Korean Assemblies of God*. Seoul: Seoul Books, 1998.

Jamir, Chongpongmeren. *The Theological Quest of an Indian Woman: Dogma, Doubts, and Debates in Pandita Ramabai's Early Christian Life*. Toronto: University of Toronto Press, 2024. https://www.cbeinternational.org/wp-content/uploads/2024/01/The-Theological-Quest-of-an-Indian-Woman.pdf.

Jenkins, Philip. *God's Continent: Christianity, Islam and Europe's Religious Crisis*. Oxford: Oxford University Press, 2007.

———. *The New Faces of Christianity: Believing the Bible in the Global South*. Oxford: Oxford University Press, 2006.

———. *The Next Christendom: The Coming of Global Christianity*. Oxford: Oxford University Press, 2011.

Jimenez-David, Rina, et al. *Towards Our Own Image: An Alternative Philippine Report on Women and Media*. Manila: Aklat Pilipino, 1985.

Johns, C. Bridges. "Pentecostals and the Praxis of Liberation: A Proposal for Subversive Theological Education." *Transformation* 11:1 (1994) 11–23.

Jorgensen, Christian K. "Mission in the Post-Modern Society." Unpublished paper, 2009.

Josephus, Flavius. *Antiquities of the Jews in the Words of Flavius Josephus*. Edinburgh: Brown and Nelson, 1828.

Kim, Yung Chung. *Women of Korea: A History from Ancient Times to 1945*. Seoul: Ewha Women's University Press, 1976.

King, J. D. "The Secret to Kathryn Kuhlman's Powerful Healing Ministry." *Charisma: The Magazine About Spirit-Led Living*, Feb. 24, 2017. https://mycharisma.com/spiritled-living/woman/the-secret-to-kathryn-kuhlman-s-powerful-healing-ministry/.

Kroeger, Catherine C. "John Chrysostom's First Homily on the Greeting to Priscilla and Aquila." *Academic Journal of CBE International: Biblical Feminism* 5:3 (1991) 15–28.

Lalitha, Jayachitra. *Re-Reading Household Relationships Christologically: Ephesians, Empire and Egalitarianism*. New Delhi: Christian World Imprints, 2017.

Langford, Joy. "Feminism and Leadership in Pentecostal Movement." *Feminist Theology* 26:1 (2017). https://journals.sagepub.com/doi/full/10.1177/0966735017714402.

Le Guin, Ursula K. "Bryn Mawr Commencement Address." In *Dancing at the Edge of the World: Thoughts on Words, Women, Places*, 4–8. New York: Grove, 1989.

Lee, Young-hoon. *The Holy Spirit Movement in Korea: Its Historical and Theological Development*. Oxford: Regnum Books International, 2009.

———. "The Life and Ministry of Dr. Yonggi Cho and Yoido Full Gospel Church." *Asian Journal of Pentecostal Studies* 7:1 (2004) 14–27.

Lewis, C. S. "Excerpts from Mere Christianity." In *Devotional Classics*, edited by Richard J. Foster and James B. Smith, 24–50. San Francisco: Harper San Francisco, 1993.

Ma, Julie C. "Asian Women and Pentecostal Ministry." In *Asian and Pentecostal: The Charismatic Face of Christianity in Asia*, edited by Allan Anderson and Edmond Tang, 129–46. Oxford: Regnum, 2005.

———. "Changing Images: Women in Asian Pentecostalism." In *Women in Pentecostal-Charismatic Leadership*, edited by Estrelda Alexander and Amos Yong, 203–14. Eugene, OR: Pickwick, 2009.

———. "Influence of Pentecostal Spirituality to Asian Christianity." *Asian Journal of Pentecostal Studies* 23:2 (2020) 107–22.

———. "The Role of Christian Women in the Global South." *Transformation: An International Journal of Holistic Mission Studies* 31:3 (2014) 194–206.

———. *When the Spirit Meets the Spirits: Pentecostal Ministry Among the Kankana-ey Tribe in the Philippines*. Frankfurt: Peter Lang, 2000.

———. "Women at Yoido Full Gospel Church: Pentecostalism in a Confucian Context." In *Human Sexuality and the Holy Spirit: Spirit-Empowered Perspective*, edited by Wonsuk Ma and Kathleen Reid-Martinez, 267–84. Tulsa, OK: Oral Roberts University Press, 2019.

Ma, Julie C., and Allan Anderson. "Pentecostals (Renewalists) 1910–2010." In *Atlas of Global Christianity*, edited by Todd M. Johnson and Kenneth R. Ross, 100–101. Edinburgh: Edinburgh University Press, 2010.

Ma, Julie C., and Wonsuk Ma. *Mission in the Spirit: Towards a Pentecostal/Charismatic Missiology*. Oxford: Regnum, 2010.

Ma, Wonsuk. "Korean: Characteristics." In *Encyclopedia of Pentecostal and Charismatic Christianity*, edited by Stanley M. Burgess, 279–81. New York: Routledge, 2006.

Mair, Jessie H. *Bungalows in Heaven: The Story of Pandita Ramabai*. London: Hurst and Blackett, 2019.

McAlpine, Thomas H. *By Word, Work, and Wonder: Cases in Holistic Mission*. Monrovia, CA: MARC, 2003.

McDonald, Margaret. *Women in Development: Viet Nam*. Manila: Asian Development Bank, 1995.

Merrill, Dean. *50 Pentecostal and Charismatic Leaders Every Christian Should Know*. Minneapolis: Chosen, 2021.

Moor, G. F. *Judaism in the First Centuries of the Christian Era, the Age of the Tannaim*. 3 vols. Peabody, MA: Hendrickson, 1997.

Murphy, Cullen. *The Word According to Eve: Women and the Bible in Ancient Times and Our Own*. New York: Penguin, 1998.

Myung, Sunghoon, and Yonggi Hong. "Church Growth and Cell Groups." In *Charis and Charisma: David Yonggi Cho and the Growth of Yoido Full Gospel Church*, edited by Myungsung Hoon and Yonggi Hong, 87–98. Oxford: Regnum, 2003.

Oberg, Maria. "'Trouble-Quiet Sowers of Unrest': Representations of Women, from Josephus to Cary." https://josephus.org/ObergJosephusandCary.htm.

Olofinjana, Israel. *20 Pentecostal Pioneers in Nigeria: Their Lives, Their Legacies*. Lagos: Enoch Adejare Adeboye Foundation, 2011.

Ook, Han-hum. "Message of Hope." In *Charis and Charisma: David Yonggi Cho and the Growth of Yoido Full Gospel Church*, edited by Myungsung Hoon and Yonggi Hong, 13–20. Oxford: Regnum, 2003.

Pagels, Elaine. *The Gnostic Gospels*. New York: Vintage, 1989.

Park, Sydney, and Kenneth Mathews. *The Post-Racial Church*. Grand Rapids: Kregel, 2011.

Pierce, Yolanda. "Woman-tology and the Future Face of Pentecostalism." *Theology Today* 68 (2012) 381–82.

Prabhu, G. Soares. "The Jesus of Faith: A Christological Contribution to an Ecumenical Third World Spirituality." In *Spirituality of the Third World*, edited by K. C. Abraham and Bernadette Mbuy-Beya, 1–23. Maryknoll, NY: Orbis, 1994.

Quisenberry, Celia. "Faith Emmanuel Benson Idahosa II: Early Life and Ministry." Jan. 13, 2025. https://astroinsightz.com/faith-emmanuel-benson-idahosa-ii/.

Radi, Heather. Introduction to *200 Australian Women: A Redress Anthology*, edited by Heather Radi, 12–15. Broadway, Australia: Women's Redress Press, 2007.

Reynolds, Annika. "Human Rights in the Age of Southeast Asian Extractivism." New Mandala, Feb. 4, 2022. https://www.newmandala.org/human-rights-in-the-age-of-southeast-asian-extractivism/.

Roebuck, David. "Go and Tell My Brother: The Waning of Women's Voices in American Pentecostalism." Paper presented at the Society for Pentecostal Studies Annual Meeting, Dallas, Texas, 1990.

Ruether, Rosemary Radford. *Sexism and God-Talk: Toward a Feminist Theology*. Boston: Beacon, 1983.

Scanzoni, Letha, and Susan Setta. "Women in Evangelical, Holiness, and Pentecostal Traditions." In *Women and Religion in America*, edited by Rosemary Radford Ruether and R. Keller, 3:250–62. San Francisco: Harper & Row, 1986.

Scott, William. "Igorot Responses to Spanish Aims: 1676–1896." *Philippine Studies* 18.4 (1971) 695–717.

Seyfferth, Anne. "First Asia-Pacific Congress of Women in Politics." Sept. 6, 2017. https://www.semanticscholar.org/paper/First-Asia-Pacific-Congress-of-Women-in-Politics-Seyfferth/7ee80f3f265dd024889a4a2475869883b410a1b9.

Shivananda, Swami. *Mukti Prayer-Bell*. Kedgaon, India: Mukti Mission Press, 1905.

The Socratic Method. "Nelson Mandela: 'Education is the most powerful weapon which you can use to change the world.'" https://www.socratic-method.com/quote-meanings/nelson-mandela-education-is-the-most-powerful-weapon-which-you-can-use-to-change-the-world.

Son, Angella. "Confucianism and the Lack of the Development of the Self Among Korean American Women." *Pastoral Psychology* 54:4 (2006) 325–35.

Spencer, Aida B. *Beyond the Curse: Women Called to Ministry*. Grand Rapids: Baker Academic, 1985.

Spittler, Russell. "Spirituality, Pentecostal and Charismatic." In *Dictionary of Pentecostal and Charismatic Movement*, edited by Stanley M. Burgess and Gary B. McGee, 800–810. Grand Rapids: Zondervan, 1988.

Sturgeon, Inez. *Give Me This Mountain*. Oakland, CA: Hunter Advertising, 1960.

Synan, Vinson. *Holiness-Pentecostal Tradition: Charismatic Movements in the Twentieth Century*. Grand Rapids: Eerdmans, 1997.

Tippett, Alan R. *People Movements in Southern Polynesia*. Chicago: Moody, 1971.

"Transformation India Movement." Patna, Bihar. https://in.linkedin.com/company/transformation-india-movement-tim.

Tucker, Ruth A. *Woman in the Maze: Questions and Answers on Biblical Equality*. Downers Grove, IL: Schenkman, 1997.

UNICEF. "Over 370 Million Girls and Women Globally Are Subjected to Rape or Sexual Assault as Children." Oct. 10, 2024. https://www.unicef.org/press-releases/over-370-million-girls-and-women-globally-subjected-rape-or-sexual-assault-children.

Valimont, Danielle. "Calcutta Mercy Ministries Overview." YouTube video, Oct. 19, 2012. www.youtube.com/watch?v=ohGiCSmIv8k.

Vanderbout, Elva. "Application for Appointment as Missionary." 1946. Mission Department Archives, Springfield, MO.

———. "Personal Newsletter to the Foreign Mission Department." March 1961. Mission Department Archives, Springfield, MO.

———. "Report on Trip to the Alsados." *The Missionary Challenge*, Oct. 1954. Mission Department Archives, Springfield, MO.

———. "Salvation-Healing Revival in Baguio City, Philippines." *Pentecostal Evangel*, Feb. 1955. Mission Department Archives, Springfield, MO.

———. "Talubin Christians Re-Enact Conversion." *The Missionary Challenge*, Aug. 1958. Mission Department Archives, Springfield, MO.

———. "A Westward Move." *In Our Missionary*, Aug. 1962. Mission Department Archives, Springfield, MO.

———. "A Work of Mercy in the Philippines." *Foreign Field Report*, Apr. 1954. Mission Department Archives, Springfield, MO.

Vellosa, Rosalee Ewell, and J. Baxter-Brown. "Changing the World, One Story at a Time: Rediscovering Evangelism." *Evangelical Review of Theology* 35:2 (2011) 100–110.

Wallis, Arthur. *God's Chosen Fast*. Fort Washington, PA: Christian Literature Crusade, 1968.

Wead, Douglas. *The Compassionate Touch*. Minneapolis: Bethany Fellowship, 1980.

Whitney, Donald. *Spiritual Disciples for the Christian Life*. Colorado Springs: NavPress, 1993.

Wikipedia. "Apostolic Faith Mission of South Africa." https://en.wikipedia.org/wiki/Talk:Apostolic_Faith_Mission_of_South_Africa.

Wimber, John, and Kevin Springer. *Power Evangelism*. New York: HarperCollins, 1984.

Yao, Xinzhong. *An Introduction to Confucianism*. Cambridge: Cambridge University Press, 2000.

Yong, Amos. Preface to *Philip's Daughters: Women in Pentecostal-Charismatic Leadership*, edited by Estrelda Alexander and Amos Yong, vii–viii. Eugene, OR: Wipf & Stock, 2009.

Yung, Hwa. *Mangoes or Bananas: The Quest for an Authentic Asian Christian Theology*. Oxford: Regnum, 2021.

Name Index

Subject Index

Note: Locators followed by "n" indicate footnotes.

Scripture Index

Acts (continued)

Romans

1 Corinthians

Galatians

Ephesians

Philippians

Colossians

2 Timothy

Philemon

James

www.ingramcontent.com/pod-product-compliance
Lightning Source LLC
LaVergne TN
LVHW050646100826
845148LV00011B/2005
9798385239184